GOD STILL ANSWERS PRAYERS

Karen Neal

God Still Answers Prayers: The Power of Prayer
Copyright © 2023 by Karen Neal

Printed in the United States of America

ISBN: 979-8-218-15752-4

Published by: Joseph's Ministry, LLC
www.josephsministryllc.com

Unless otherwise identified, Scripture quotations are from the King James Version. Copyright © 1982 by Thomas Nelson, Inc. Used by permission. All rights reserved.

All rights reserved. This book or any portion thereof may not be reproduced or used in any manner whatsoever without the express written permission of the publisher except for the use of brief quotations in a book review.

Table of Contents

Introduction…………………………………………………...5

A Call to Prayer……………………………………………….7

Scriptures……………………………………………………...117

Salvation Prayer………………………………………………169

About the Author………………………………………….......171

Introduction

There are different kinds of prayers. If it ever was a time to pray, it is now. There are all kinds of evil in this world, and it appears that it is increasing. The Lord said evil would wax worse and worse. He also noted that perilous times would come, but God tells us to redeem the time. If it ever was a time to pray, it is now. We must increase our prayer life; spend more time seeking the Lord God. Men are always to pray and not faint. Scripture verse says we are to pray without ceasing. We should always be in an attitude of prayer. We will pray more in the Holy Ghost or the Spirit. We should spend more time praying in the Holy Ghost, building ourselves on our most Holy faith.

Note: The words in this book were downloaded from God on June 28, 2013, while I was sitting in my backyard.

> *Scripture References*
> *Romans 8:26*
> *Jude 1:20*
> *1 Thessalonians 5:16-18*
> *Luke 18:1*

A Call to Prayer

Pray in the Holy Spirit. By praying in the Spirit, you are praying the absolute perfect will of God, for He prays the mind of the Father and the will of the Father. I will say something so profound, but it is a revelation from the Lord. All Prophets are intercessors, but not all Intercessors are Prophets or Prophetesses. If studying the Old Testament particularly, we must become serious about the things of God. Prayer is work; it is discipline. In the Old Testament, God wanted to destroy them when they came out of Egypt, but Moses stood in the gap as their Intercessor, and God spared them.

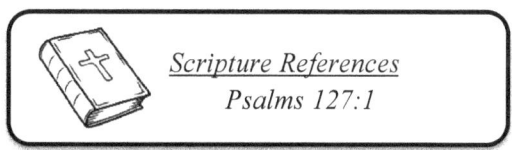
Scripture References
Psalms 127:1

God is the I am. He is whatever you need Him to be. He will heal if you need Him to heal you, for He is Jehovah Rapha. He is your provider, Jehovah Jireh. El Shaddai, the God, that's more than enough.

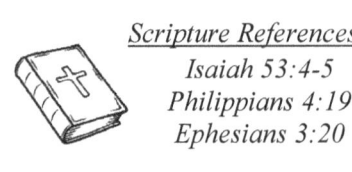

Scripture References
Isaiah 53:4-5
Philippians 4:19
Ephesians 3:20

God is going to sanctify His church. The Holy Ghost's fire will burn up the chaff and the dross. Jesus is returning for a glorious church without a spot or a blemish. God told Joshua to sanctify the people, for tomorrow, I will do wonders among them. I say this; God is going to do wonders among us. We need to allow God to take something out of our lives and put something into our lives. These children are for signs and wonders.

There is going to be a transfer of wealth. The wealth of the wicked is laid up for the just. If it ever was a time for a financial breakthrough to get this Gospel to the nations, it is now. I believe God will supernaturally and divinely provide for His people.

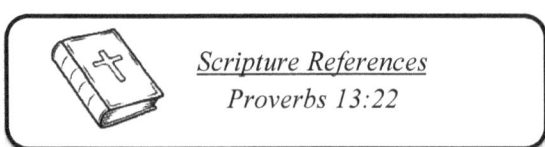

Scripture References
Proverbs 13:22

There are many people that God has prepared for the nations. God calls us to go to the world, for we need the finances to get there.

I have gone to many countries, but I believe God wants to send me continuously to other nations. Some nations have begged me to come. But I need more resources to go. I could go to that nation every month or every other month if the resources were there. I have heard people say where God guides, He provides. I also know that people often won't obey the Lord's voice or the Holy Spirit's leading. I believe it's time to get this Gospel out to the world with all of my heart. Paul said that Satan had hindered him, but I will come at a more opportune time.

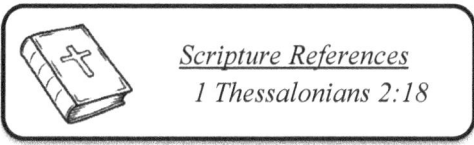

Scripture References
1 Thessalonians 2:18

Jesus said the end would not come until the Gospel of the Kingdom had been preached to all nations. Jesus said He would not return until the restoration of all things.

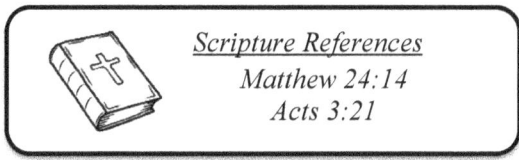

Scripture References
Matthew 24:14
Acts 3:21

The first transfer of wealth was with the church in the wilderness. That is when God delivered the children of Israel out of

Egypt. God told them to borrow gold and silver from the Egyptians. That was the Sovereign head of the Lord to have the Israelites go to the Egyptians, and they released their wealth unto them. Praise the Lord. Amen. I believe God is going to do it again. The glory of the latter house is greater than that of the former house. Meditate on that scripture, and it will reveal other things as well.

God told Joshua every tread of ground that your feet shall tread upon, that have I given unto you. He said He would provide us with houses we did not build, filled with good things. He said He would give us the hidden treasure of darkness. God tells us to get wisdom and, with knowledge, get understanding. Wealth and riches are on the one hand, and long life is on the other. God talks about being a good steward of what God has given us. Are we good stewards at the level we are at now? God tells us to despise not our small beginnings; continue to thank God and trust Him. There are more incredible things He will do. I have been in that situation before, but God always comes to bring you to a wealthy place and will do it again.

"Jesus Christ, the same yesterday, today, and forever."

Hebrews 13:8

God does not change. God has done so much for me through the years. I remember buying my first home with three children in my twenties. It was a lovely home, and I could pay cash to furnish it fully. I brought the furniture with me when my job transferred me, and I was relocated. It was a good job. I already had ten years of seniority there, but you lose your seniority when you move.

Getting back to the furniture, I have not seen anything that I like or would enjoy any better than what I had in the same furniture. It was packaged and transferred well. I know God will restore everything, and it will be better. Some of you, as I have, trust in the Lord; He will restore. So many of you have lost much but believe God to restore you.

If God blesses you with wealth and riches, would you still seek the Kingdom of God first and allow Him to be your everything? Would you still desire to live holy? Would you still want to be more like Jesus? Those are some things you would like to ponder in your heart. Can you still walk and live humbly before the Lord? Would you still give Him the glory and the praise for everything He has done, is doing, and will do? God has said, we are kings and priests unto him. We are a royal priesthood, a Holy people. A peculiar people.

Scripture References
Job 22:28
John 10:10
Ephesians 3:20

In the Bible, Jesus gave His servants talents. He gave five to one, two to another, and to another, He gave one. The servants with the five and two talents made investments with them and doubled their investment. But the one given one talent buried it and did not invest it, and Jesus rebuked him. We should never despise small beginnings. If God is paying your light bill and keeping your lights on because you didn't have a job, be thankful for that. Be grateful if He keeps a roof over your head and provides clothes and food. Forget about what people are saying. Keep your eyes on Jesus and keep confessing and believing in God. Let go and just let God's will be done.

Malachi 3:10-11 tells us to bring all the tithes into the storehouse and see if God does not pour out a blessing on us where we do not have enough room to receive it. God promises to open the windows of Heaven. We need to remember to give the tenth percent as tithe and offerings. God also talks about him that is scattered but yet increased.

Psalms 8:25 says I have never seen the righteous forsaken nor his seed begging for bread. Sometimes, we have to do without something if we have gotten into debt. To make sure that we can give. Giving and receiving is love; it's a principle.

God said there would be seedtime and harvest as long as the Earth remains. There is winter, summer, spring, and fall. Every seed produces after its kind. Isaac seeded in the land of famine and reaped a hundredfold.

It is not how much you have; keep giving. You may not have much to offer, but you still give like the widow woman with the two mite. The Lord talks about coming empty-handed before. We have never gone empty-handed before the Lord. We must work on getting out of debt. We should do everything we can to get out of debt and pay our bills. Don't despise small beginnings ever.

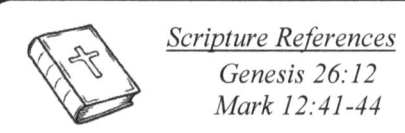

Scripture References
Genesis 26:12
Mark 12:41-44

Trust God to get you out of debt supernaturally. I have been debt-free before, except for my home. Some say that if God can get it through you, He will get it to you. There is a lot of truth in that, but you have many people who say that they know people who have come to them that were in great need. All they say is, I will pray for you. As a single parent and woman, I have been able to help and feed people. To God be the glory. Sometimes, we don't see things like God sees things. Our thoughts are not His thoughts.

"For my thoughts are not your thoughts, neither are your ways my ways, saith the Lord."

Isaiah 55:8 KJV

I remember I was at a conference in Tulsa, and I was standing in the back. While the speaker was speaking, I went to sit in the lobby. A woman came out and said, "Okay, it's you. I remember when you used to feed me. I had three children at that time." I would go into my refrigerator and cabinet and give her food. At the time, I didn't think anything of it. I saw someone in need, and so I helped. She said, "I am married now and buying my own home." What a blessing.

She could have said how the meeting was and how the glory of the Lord would manifest. Instead, she said, "You would have prayer and Bible study in your home." She thought about how I helped her. She wasn't the only one; there were others. God does not forget. A man may forget, but God does not forget. Neither does He forget our labor of love. God said all labor is profitable.

When the glory of the Lord comes in a place, you will see God move in a sovereign way like never before. It will be the sovereign hand of God. I believe this. We are headed for the most remarkable revival we have ever seen in these last days. We are getting ready to see some glorious things happen. Things that we have never seen before, by the hand of the Lord. To God be the glory. People, get ready! Prepare yourselves. Sanctify yourselves. Get ready for restoration in your life and transition like never before. For we have the treasures in earthen vessels. God said some to honor and some to dishonor.

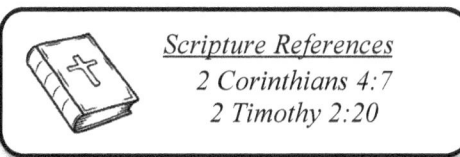

Scripture References
2 Corinthians 4:7
2 Timothy 2:20

God's glory will be seen upon us. But gross darkness will cover the Earth. God wants His glory to be seen upon you. Don't be discouraged. If you are in debt, trust God. Cut back and stop charging so much with credit cards. God said we have not because we ask not. Sometimes, we have to knock. Keep on knocking. Keep on seeking. We must press until the manifestation or answer comes.

We go from victory to victory, faith to faith, glory to glory, and strength to strength. There are levels of glory in every one of these things I mentioned. I know that God is faithful, and He never changes. He will never change. There will be a transition in the church spiritually, but there will also be a transition into the supernatural. God is going to bless. He will get the glory.

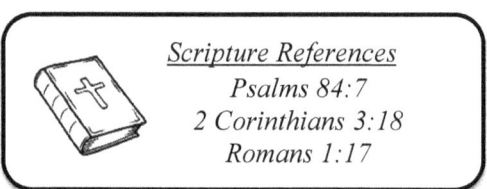

Scripture References
Psalms 84:7
2 Corinthians 3:18
Romans 1:17

When I was in Paris, France, a door opened for me to participate in a Pastor's crusade from Dominica. Unfortunately, I needed a car to make that meeting. I was the singer and Minister for the team. While I was looking for another Lincoln Town car, a businessman had a Mercedes Benz for sale. I looked at it and found that it was a lovely car. It was not a Lincoln Town car like I originally wanted, but God knows better than we know. I talked with the businessman, and he said it was in excellent condition. Then he said I could take it for a test drive and that it was okay for me to take the car home overnight. I was extremely hesitant to take the car home, but ultimately, I did.

The next day, I took the car to a mechanic. He said the vehicle was in great shape, with only a few minor things that needed to be done. That's when I decided to purchase the car. God had already given me the money to pay cash for the vehicle. I praise God that I did not have to pay a car note. To God be the glory. I was also able to purchase the Lincoln Town car simultaneously. God is good! Even if you desire something, God will give it to you.

I believe in holiness and living a godly life. I know that's the perfect will of God. God has done some beautiful things in my life. Sometime later, I purchased a small home. Praise the Lord. That Benz was the best car ever. Also, I bought an excellent Volvo. I found out that all Mercedes cars are different. But God knew that I would need that car to travel the nation. I have gone from state to state and have never broken down on the highway. Praise the Lord. It's an old

Mercedes; as a matter of fact, an antique now. Unfortunately, someone hit my car and totaled it out. But God will restore, I believe, seven times better. I have driven that car for about fifteen years.

Praise the Lord. I have seen some beautiful things that God has done. I have seen people saved and families delivered. I know that businesses were birthed in prayer. I used to have all-night prayers on Friday nights. I believe in all-night prayers. Jesus prayed all night, and so did the early church. In the Bible, Jacob worked for his uncle Laban, a very unjust and unfair man. This man was so dishonest to Jacob. Jacob was in love with Rachel, Laban's younger daughter, and had to work seven years for her. But Laban did not give Rachel to be his wife but gave Leah, his older daughter. So, he tricked Jacob into marrying his older daughter. But Jacob was so in love with Rachel that he was willing to work seven more years for her. But Jacob decided to leave, not having much due to Laban's dishonesty.

God told Jacob what to do with the animals. Jacob said all the striped or spotted animals would come with him, so Laban agreed. God told Jacob to take a reed and make it striped or spotted and put it before their eyes. Then, when the animals come to the brook to drink and give birth, they would be that color. Well, that was precisely what happened. Jacob was made very wealthy at that time. He left, but they came after him. But he was able to escape. Praise the Lord. God can give you creative ideas or wealthy inventions to prosper you to make you wealthy or rich. God is a creator or inventor. He holds all power in His hands. If it's not there, God can create it.

Matthew 19:26 states, "With God, all things are possible." God is still working miracles and working in the supernatural. The closer it gets to the coming of Jesus' return and the appearance of the antichrist, we will have to believe in God's supernatural ability. One of the prophets or kings said, is anything too hard for God? My God is able, and He won't fail. There is no failure with God.

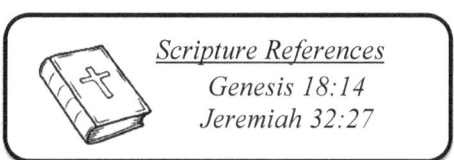

Scripture References
Genesis 18:14
Jeremiah 32:27

When Jesus got ready to pay His taxes, He told Peter to go fishing, and he found a coin in the fish's mouth. He took that and paid the taxes. God is fantastic and has not changed. Peter, by trade, was a fisherman, but he was not catching any fish. So, Jesus told Peter to cast the net on the other side of the boat for a catch. There were so many fish that it began to break or tear the net. I have learned that it will always come to pass when God speaks or works. Praise God, glory to God! Some of you will have good prophecies over your life.

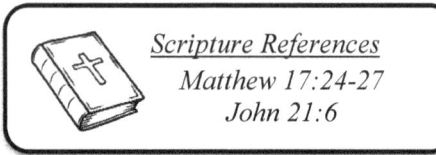

Scripture References
Matthew 17:24-27
John 21:6

Timothy does warfare with those prophecies. We must believe God in this hour like never before. Glory to God for His goodness and His faithfulness. To God be the glory for the great things He has done.

Abraham was so rich and had so much that he and Lot disagreed. Abraham said they should separate; therefore, Lot and Abraham went their separate ways. Lot took the greener land or property, and God made Abraham rich. God blessed Abraham and made him a blessing. You can go through the Bible and find men and women God blessed. Even in this time, some men and women had endured incredible hardships, but God blessed them. Even in our times, God is working miracles.

I remember this lady wanted to buy her dream home, but they wanted sixteen thousand as a down payment. She did not have the money. The Word of the Lord came through me. She had to have it in two weeks. She had no way of getting it. She said somebody gave her ten thousand dollars ($10,000), and then her brother loaned her the other six thousand dollars. She was waiting on her house to sell, but it didn't. I believe God is going to do some incredible things in this hour. God did it for the children of Israel. He supernaturally took care of His people. God will provide. I also believe that God will shake everything that can be shaken, and only the things of God will remain.

"Judgment will start in the house of God, then the world."

1 Peter 4:17

"It is God that giveth us the power to get wealth, that he may establish his covenant."

Deuteronomy 8:18

God is a covenant, God. We have a better covenant than the children of Israel or the Old Testament.

"My God shall supply all my needs, according to His riches in glory by Christ Jesus."

Philippians 4:19

God promised us that He would give us gold as dust.

"We should study to show thyself approved, a workman that needeth not to be ashamed, rightly dividing the word of truth."

2 Timothy 2:15 KJV

We must get an understanding of the things of God.

"Get wisdom, and with wisdom, gain understanding."

Proverbs 4:7

"My covenant will I not break, nor alter the thing that is gone out of my lips."

Psalms 89:34

"Then shalt thou lay up gold as dust, and the gold of Ophir as the stones of the brooks. Yea, the Almighty shall be thy defence, and thou shalt have plenty of silver."

Job 22:24-25

" Trust in the Lord with all thine heart; and lean not unto thine own understanding."

Proverbs 3:5

We must continue studying God's Word and rightfully divide God's Word to increase wisdom and knowledge to renew our minds. We must get the mind of Christ. Good things are happening. I desire to be right in the middle of God's will. I pray that you do as well. Desire to walk in His ways to know His will and do His will. God's angels will encamp all around us. They will be there to help us and to see us through until the end. God is Jehovah.

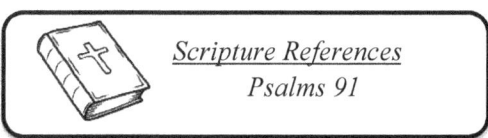

Scripture References
Psalms 91

He that hath left houses, fathers, mothers with persecutions will no wise receive a hundredfold in this life. Only some people can claim this scripture. I can and others as well, but I have gone through a lot of persecution in my walk with God, especially since I decided to obey God. I have some things coming to me, and some of you also. Trust God because He will provide. Ask of me, and I will give the kingdom and the uttermost part of the earth for thy possession. We should be taking over property and souls. He that winneth souls are wise.

> *Scripture References*
> Mark 10:29
> Psalms 2:8
> Proverbs 11:30

Christ hath redeemed us from the law's curse, but we need money to get this Gospel out. I have gone to many nations. I am anointed for the nations. I don't need to ask for open doors; they are already open. To God be the glory. When Abraham went to get Lot, he took his armed and trained men to get him. Abraham taught his men to be warriors. They were skilled men. Likewise, King David had men that were discontented and in debt. These men had problems. They were in a cave, but King David trained these men to be warriors and to believe in God, worshippers, and praisers of God. These men became great warriors. They prospered and were powerful men. When they got ready to build the temple, they gave hundreds of millions of dollars to help build Solomon's temple. It was more than twenty billion dollars that King David gave towards constructing the temple.

We had some Ministers give not only to prosper themselves but also to teach God's people to prosper and do warfare against the forces of darkness. We must learn to confess God's Word in faith and believe God for miracles that supernaturally prosper and bless us. Some Ministers have deliberately robbed God's people of their finances. When these people go through a test, a trial, or a crisis, all they can do is say, I will pray for you, and most of the time, they won't even do that.

> *Scripture References*
> *Galatians 3:13*
> *Genesis 14*
> *1 Samuel 22:2*
> *1 Kings 6*
> *1 Chronicles 29*

I remember I had Bible study and prayer in my home. The people that regularly came did not ask for prayer for finances. I taught my people the Word of the Lord by revelation knowledge of the Holy Spirit in life in glory. People would come into the house and need healing. If they came once or twice, they got healed. Whatever the need was, God met the need supernaturally. I believe I walked in glory. I also think God allowed it. I believe it is for the latter-day church. The five-fold ministry gifts are perfect. The church and for the work of the ministry. How will you effectively minister to others when you need to be taught yourself? I remember God told me to go into the byways and the highways and compel them to come into my house. I saw a lot of miracles during that time of ministry, and I still do; I praise the Lord. To God be the glory!

"And he gave some apostles, some prophets, some evangelist and some pastors and teachers; For the perfecting of the saints, for the work of the ministry, for the edifying of the body of Christ."

Ephesians 4:11-12

I remember that over thirty years ago, God told me, "I would not share my glory with no man," when I was being trained for ministry by God. I have never forgotten that; I may never forget that as long as I live. God is faithful. I remember when I would read and study God's word; it was so real to me. It was as if God was talking to me Himself. I remember sometimes He would be so strong in my life. I would be reading the word, and revelations were so alive. It was like God was talking to me Himself. Sometimes, I must put the Bible down and praise and worship the Lord. Then I would go back and study it again. God is fantastic; He has great things in store for His church.

I believe the church has been in transition. Most people need to learn how to move or transition to the next. A lot of the change will also be in the financial arena. Some people are satisfied with just having their needs met. Others, God has blessed us to go further. But believe it or not, there are many selfish people out there. Greed, jealousy, and covetousness are in the church. But when you walk in the spirit, you will not fulfill the lust of the flesh. For we walk by faith and not by sight. The just shall live by faith. We are overcomers.

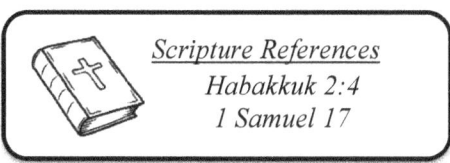

Scripture References
Habakkuk 2:4
1 Samuel 17

No matter what the enemy does. We are winners. We cannot think of thoughts of defeat and expect to be winners. We cannot feel like a wimp and expect to be champions. King David was a champion. He thought like a champion. He told Goliath, I have killed the lions and bear, and I will take your head off and feed your carcass to the fowl of the air. King David was not cowardly. We must stay fierce. King David refused when Saul wanted King David to put his armor on. It was unfamiliar to him. King David told Goliath, you come to me with swords and shields, and I come to you in the name of the Lord. There is power in the name of Jesus. Is there not a cause?

The church also has weapons: The name of Jesus, the Word of the Lord, the blood of Jesus, the gifts of the Spirit, and the fruits of the Spirit. All of these are weapons put forth to us to put on Christ. You ask what these have to do with prayer. We will need everything I have said, for the enemy will not let the church prosper that quickly. We will fight the good fight of faith and win in every area. You look at men like Dr. Yongi Cho, who didn't own a car or a bicycle to ride. He started believing in God for a bike and a cherry wood desk. I believe he saw himself with it, and God gave it to him.

Proverbs 29:18 say that where there is no vision, the people perish. You should see yourself as rich to help others, and your family gets the Gospel. Can you see yourself in a better home? Driving a better car? In better health? Fulfilling your destiny and purpose on Earth? Can you see yourself living long, finishing strong, dying great, not just having worry inside you? Leaving a legacy for your family and the church? Will you be one who will be able to say, like Paul, I have finished my course; I have fought the good fight of faith?

There is laid up for me, a crown of righteousness. You know I have dealt with a lot of persecution. I remember the Lord said that all that live godly in Christ Jesus shall suffer persecution. It is not might, but you shall. This was so real to me. Jesus said if they did it to a green tree, what would they do to a dry tree? No matter how challenging the trial is, stay focused. I remember years ago when God told me I would win if I didn't quit. I will say this: I have spent much time with God and still do.

God speaks, but are we listening? Can we hear His voice? There are many voices out there. But God said, My sheep hear My voice, and a stranger they will not hear. Jesus said I do what I see my Father do. Jesus spoke the word to defeat the devil. Get ready for miracles and the supernatural power of God in every area.

Scripture References
2 Timothy 3:12
2 Timothy 4:8
Luke 23:31
John 5:19
John 10:27-28

When I was praying about the ministry, I remember it came to mind, disciples of Christ. While training them to be disciples, I remember that since I have been in Tulsa, the Lord said, "you took care of my people long ago." Then I went to their meeting, and a woman was ministering. I was going to hear the Word of the Lord. I remember the words, "Come up here, beautiful lady." I was the first person she called up. The Lord spoke through her and said, "Thanks a million, thanks a million. You took care of My people." I could not help but weep. The Lord had just spoken that to me. God is real. He is alive. Praise God for Jesus.

If you study the life of King David, he was a warrior. When they burned Ziklag and took his wives, children, wealth, and possessions, they wept until there were no more tears. But the same men that King David trained and saw all the mighty acts and deeds that he had accomplished, with God's help, wanted to stone him, but King David went and sought the Lord. God told King David to go and recover all. Hallelujah!! Praise the Lord!! (1 Samuel 30 KJV)

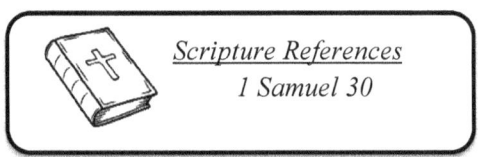

Scripture References
1 Samuel 30

All you need is a word from the Lord. King David found the men who had burned the city and took their wives, children, and possessions. Some men got sick, so King David left them with the stuff. The others went with King David. They met one of the soldiers. He was ill, so King David asked him where the men were. He told King David to promise that he would not kill him. So, he told King David where they were. King David went in, won the battle, and got his wife back, his possessions, his children, and the other men's possessions. He then got all his treasures, gold and silver, and possessions. King David had recovered all. Just as the word of the Lord hath spoken to him. Some of the men did not want to share with the men left behind because they were weak and sick to travel, so they stayed with their possessions. But King David called some men belial because they did not want to share equally. But King David said all would share equally. Jesus, Himself, said that in the Gospel.

In Revelation 2:2 KJV, Jesus, said you know those that are Apostles and those that are not. In the church, there were Prophets and Teachers. Phillip had four daughters who were Prophetesses.

Jehoshaphat had this group of people coming against them; He sought the Lord. He sent Judah before him, and they praised the Lord and did not have to fight with weapons, but they praised the Lord and won the battle. They said the Lord is good, and His mercy endures forever. They thought a large army was coming against them, so they trampled one another. Many of them were killed; some fled. They spent three days gathering the spoils. Some of us have great battles, even in our finances, but now is the time for a breakthrough. It's not enough to win the fight. It's time for the great spoil. For some of us, God is going to make us rich. God made Abraham very rich. We can also walk in the Abrahamic covenant. But we have a better covenant now that Jesus has come, died and is resurrected.

Galatians 3:13 says that God's promises are yea and amen. Christ has redeemed us from the curse of the law that the blessing of Abraham might come upon us. Poverty is a curse. Jesus did say the poor would be with you always. In Acts, when Ananias and Sapphira sold their properties, they both lied to the Holy Spirit. They both dropped dead, and they took them out to bury them. There was unity in the church. The church moved in power and authority in miracles and signs and wonders. When they lied to the Holy Spirit, it broke something in the realm of the spirit. We are all to say the same thing.

Don't take your dreams and visions to the grave. Let's believe in God and trust God like never before. Be history makers. We made history in China. Praise God. I know that I was in the perfect will of God. We went to a nation of communist China, and no Christians had been there in over fifty years. That nation was open unto us. Praise the Lord. To God be the glory for the great things He is doing.

> *Scripture References*
> Acts 21:9
> 2 Chronicles 20
> Acts 5:1-11
> 1 Corinthians 1:10

King David also helped or gave to other people. When King David gets blessed, he blesses a lot of people. Until today, that is still an ordinance in Israel. The way King David did with his men and blessed the people. Think about that. In the New Testament of the church, they had all things in common. Many sold properties and houses and laid the profit at the Apostles' feet. Not so they can do something just for the church and ministers, but every person can be blessed. There is a pattern to the church. The Apostles and the Prophets are a significant part of that pattern.

We should walk in the power and authority that God desires for the church to walk in until we follow the way God has for the church. Peter and the other Apostles would not leave prayer and would go to wait on tables or take care of the needs of people. But they stayed in the word and prayer. The church was built on the

Apostles, Prophets, and Jesus Christ, the chief, and head cornerstone. Praise the Lord. Glory to God. I trust the Apostles and Prophets and Prophetesses will come forth.

They complained about the person coming in the previous hour and getting the same pay. Jesus mentioned they were hardhearted, but his heart was good or different. Can you see why God said King David was a man after His heart? King David was a man that sought the Lord, but he was also a worshiper; he knew God. King David was a Prophet, a Priest, and a King. There is a place in the Bible where King David told them to bring his ephod. Only the priest was allowed to wear the ephod. The priest could do things not even the king was allowed to do. But King David could function in all those capacities. So God said we are kings and priests unto Him.

Remember, when the thief has been caught, he has to restore sevenfold. God has also talked about the sixty-and-a-hundredfold return. God has also said a thousand times more. I was singing praise to God and encouraging the people. God's glory is incredible. God's glory will be revealed. His glory shall be seen upon His people. Thy will be done, thy kingdom come. Amen.

> *Scripture References*
> Acts 6:21
> Ephesians 2:20
> Matthew 28:12
> 1 Samuel 30:7
> Acts 6:2
> Proverbs 6:31
> Matthew 13:8
> Mark 4:20
> Deuteronomy 1:11
> Matthew 6
> 1 Samuel 30:7-22

Dr. Yongi Cho's church is powerful. They are people of prayer. There is a place called Prayer Mountain in South Korea. Constant prayer is going on. He has a church with seven hundred thousand people: over fifty thousand millionaires. On my way to Paris, France, on a missionary journey, and to other nations, I had an opportunity to sit beside a businessperson from Dr. Choi's church. We had a lovely conversation about the things of God. He was on a business trip. That trip was also fantastic. The glory of the Lord filled the church; the Heavens were opened. As I encouraged the people and sang God's praises, the glory of the Lord came upon me and then filled the church. I saw something I had never seen before or since. Every person in the church was praising God, and demons were crying out. Some were worshiping, and some were bowing. It was something to behold. One woman said she was the highest God, the spirit of the antichrist.

God is awesome. You could see the glory in the picture that Mother Boyd had. That was the second time I saw the glory revealed in an image. The first time I saw it was with Mother Boyd's relative she had taken in. I was in a Prophetess meeting on the South side of town. I had a word of the Lord.

I saw people praying, a lot of people. I felt strange on the inside. I hope the church voluntarily prays and does not wait for a disaster or emergency. I trust the Lord for the spirit of prayer to come upon the church. God said, my house shall be called a house of prayer. Our bodies are the temple of the Holy Spirit. The early church was a praying church. God said to contend for the faith once given among the Saints. The Saints who God describes were praying people. They knew how to pray the prayer of faith, hear from Heaven, and get miracles. They knew how to walk in the supernatural power of God, revive their dead, have miracles, have their needs met, and healing for their bodies. Hannah was a mighty woman of God who sought the Lord day and night. So was the Prophetess Anna.

Jesus is coming for them that are looking for His appearance. But we must occupy until He comes; we must keep the faith. God will raise in the body of Christ, Apostles, Prophets, and Prophetess.

> *Scripture References*
> Matthew 21:12-14
> Jude 1:3
> Luke 19:13-15
> 2 Corinthians 6:19-20

He is going to give some people large sums of money. Some people are to be givers in the body of Christ. I know I am a giver. Sometimes, the enemy will fight givers hard, but you must press your way forward. You have to push your way. Paul said, "I press for the prize of the high calling in Christ Jesus." Paul fought many battles to finish his course; he fought the good fight of faith. We must do the same to finish our course and finish strong.

David said to teach us to number our days. We have to trust the Lord to live long and finish strong. But we must learn to endure hardship as good soldiers. Remember Philippians 4:13, "*I can do all things through Christ that strengthens me.*" We must have the strength of the Lord.

Romans 8:28 says that all things work together for your good; for those called according to His purpose. Whatever the devil means for evil, the Lord will work it for our good. In the hour that we're living, we must be sensitive to the voice of the Lord. God will give us directions and instructions, and we must do it precisely the way God has said and not how we want it done, or someone tells us to do it. We must become one with God. That can be done by spending time with God in prayer. Sometimes just meditating upon the word both day and night, then shall we make our way, prosper and have success.

When I was in Brussels, Belgium, I remember they were praying for an old warrior who himself is a general in the Lord's army. At the conference in Brussels, Belgium, the old warrior prayed for God to raise generals in his service. He said you are a general, and you look like a general. To God be the glory. Praise God. Thank you, Jesus. If we are to become anything at all, it's by the grace of Jesus Christ. God is building his army for the latter days. Every missionary journey that I have taken has been a prosperous journey. To God be the glory. They wanted me to come to China and Paris, France, within two months. They wanted me to minister at a women's conference.

Thank you, Jesus, for your goodness and your favor. I also believe God's favor will increase as we go forth to do God's work. Also, believe that the ministering spirit and Angels help us fulfill what God has called us to do.

> *Scripture References*
> Philippians 3:13
> Psalms 90:12-17
> Nehemiah 8:10
> Joshua 1:8

There is only a window of opportunity left to reach some nations. After that, other doors are going to open. We will have to know the perfect timing of the Lord, the suitable time. Think about that. We must know when it is for us to transition or shift to the next level. Also, we must understand the next phase of ministry. Also, we must know when to go from a job to starting our business.

We must understand and have the revelation of the power of praise and worship like never before. Some of us will give Jesus praise because of what He has already done. Not only has He blessed us through the years with material blessings, but also what he has done for us spiritually. So our eyes are going to be opened.

Psalms 149 says that we need to meditate on that whole Psalms. It is powerful. Praise still or stop the enemy. God binds nobles for our sake when we praise the Lord. God is working behind the scenes. That is in the realm of the spirit. Writing this book has blessed me. I hope you will be as blessed reading it. Also, God will increase your revelation of Him and His word. Jesus is Lord of Lords and King of Kings. Amen.

In Acts of the Apostle, Cornelius was of the Italian band; he was a Gentile who gave to the poor and needy. God sent Peter to Cornelius' house to preach the Gospel to him, and his household was saved. So we are getting ready to see household salvation; it's not only because you give to five ministers but also to those in need. Cornelius gave alms to the poor.

Jesus made sure Cornelius' household was saved. Peter fell into a trance on the rooftop and saw four-footed beasts. He said he did not touch anything unclean. So, Jesus told Peter, don't call unclean that which I have cleansed.

Gentiles were called dogs in the Bible. God will give instructions to some people on where to go or some people what to do. You are going to have the finances to do it. Please obey the Lord.

God is getting ready to do some unseen things. Amen. Praise the Lord. Remember, your money has a purpose. Be a good steward.

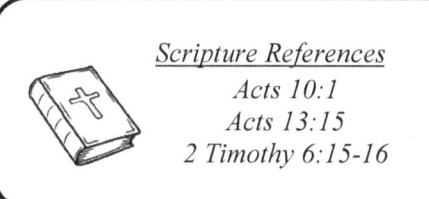

Scripture References
Acts 10:1
Acts 13:15
2 Timothy 6:15-16

Luke 18:1 is the story of the widow and unjust judge. Men are always to pray and not faint. This woman did not give up; she continued to hear and ask the judge. She did not give up until she got her answer. The judge did not regard God or man. But he did give the widow what she wanted. He said less she continually weary me. Sometimes you seek and keep on seeking, ask and keep on asking, knock and keep on knocking. Then keep on praising God until the answer comes. Amen.

Psalms 149 tells the Church, the victory is ours. The power of praise stills or stops the enemy. I believe the church will have the revelation of praise and the power of praise in a more remarkable way. God is an awesome God, and His spirit moves him. Mountains are going to move in our lives. God will also help those who have lost everything or what the enemy has stolen, as God spoke through the Prophet Joel. God said to the Prophet Isaiah that none says restore, but he will restore.

According to Proverbs 6:31, when the thief has been caught, he has to restore sevenfold. Some people that will read this book have had much stolen from them. Some people have lost hope of ever receiving or having what the enemy has stolen from them. However, after reading this book, some of you will have your hope restored and will be determined to believe in God for restoration, especially in your prayer life and reading the Word of the Lord. Some have even had people pray evil prayers against you for witchcraft.

But remember, no one or nothing can curse who God has blessed. Break the power of those words with the name of Jesus and the Word of the Lord. While in prayer, some of you can transition or shift into places where God is ordaining you to walk in. Some of you will go to your next level in prayer, strength, glory, and faith. Don't give up; keep pressing. The breakthrough will come, and God will honor our faithfulness. Don't worry about false friends and false prophets, teachers, apostles, and brethren.

In 2 Timothy 2:15 it says that we should study to show yourselves approved. A workman that needs not be ashamed rightfully dividing the word of truth. We should anchor ourselves in the word and prayer. The Holy Spirit we have received will teach us everything and guide us into all truths. We have the most excellent teacher, comforter, counselor, and helper inside us. You know there is a saying by the saints of old that failure is a prayer failure. The saints of Christ. Paul said he prayed until they were born into the kingdom of God, and he travailed until Christ was formed in them. Unless we pray and study the word, we will not be able to stand. We will not be able to endure hardness as good soldiers. God has promised that His people would not be made ashamed. I know from experience there are all kinds of prayers. I have had the privilege of praying all kinds of prayers. But when we pray in the Holy Ghost, it will always be God's perfect prayer and will because the spirit prays the will of God and the mind of God.

Scripture References
Isaiah 42:22
Genesis 12:1-3
1 Chronicles 16:22
Galatians 4:9
Isaiah 54:4
Romans 10:11
Joel 2:26-27

So when you don't know how to pray, pray in the Holy Ghost or tongues. Sometimes the Holy Ghost may even awaken you at night. Just pray to the perfect will of God by praying in the Holy Ghost. As I said earlier in the book, I was in a meeting and told them what I saw. I saw a lot of people praying all over the world. I know that God will bring it to pass. I understand that some people did not receive the Word of the Lord. Nevertheless, it was the Word of the Lord, and it shall come to pass. God said in Amos 3:7, He will do nothing on the Earth until he shows it first to his servants, the prophets.

"Believe the Lord so shall ye be established; believe his prophets, so shall ye prosper."

2 Chronicles 20:20

The church is built upon the apostles and prophets. Jesus Christ is the chief head cornerstone.

Ephesians 2:20

In the lives of prophets, you will find they talked a lot about Jesus. Paul said I preach nothing else but Jesus Christ and him crucified. Jesus spoke of Abraham; Abraham saw my day as a prophet himself. When God asked Abraham to sacrifice his son Isaac, he told them we would go but would return. When Abraham was ready to slay Isaac, the angel held his hand. There was a ram caught in the thicket. There, Abraham called God Jehovah Jireh. God will provide. I believe it was there that Abraham saw the day of Jesus Christ, the Lamb, to be slain for the world. Jesus talked about it in John. God is awesome. Jesus was the Lamb that was slain from the very foundation of the world.

We must return to the apostles' doctrine and the early Christians' actions. We must contend for the faith that was once given among the Saints. If we pray, get into the word, and sanctify ourselves, we will see miracles and the supernatural power of God. The glory of the latter house will be greater than that of the former house. I can sense it in the atmosphere.

> *Scripture References*
> *John 8:56-59*
> *Genesis 22:11-12*
> *Jude 1:3*
> *Haggai 2:9*

Faith cometh by hearing and hearing by the Word of the Lord according to Romans 10:17. There may be sick people in the body of

Christ, but we are going to see some of the greatest miracles we have ever seen in our lives. I am a walking miracle myself. Praise God. To God be the glory. Get ready; revelations will increase, and the gifts of the spirit will grow. The apostles and prophets will take their rightful place in the Kingdom of God. Until the apostles and prophets take their place in the body of Christ, the body of Christ will not be able to operate in the power and authority that God has called the church to operate in His kingdom. The righteous are as bold as a lion. God told the Prophet, Jeremiah, don't be afraid of their faces; less he would confound him before them. He told Jeremiah to root out, pluck up, tear down, and build back up. The same false teachings that will be rooted out plucked up, and then torn down will build back up with the truth.

There will be apostolic and prophetic prayers that will be prayed by the inspiration of the Holy Ghost. God is calling his intercessors and the body of Christ to pray. Many will find themselves waking up in the middle of the night. Just pray, those of you baptized in the Holy Ghost, pray more in the spirit; indeed, you can also pray with an understanding. Sometimes even in the spirit, you may find yourself praying the same thing repeatedly. Stay with the Holy Ghost until the spirit releases you, then continually flow with the spirit, whether with praise or praying with your understanding.

The apostles asked the Lord to teach them to pray. The disciples knew that Jesus was a praying man. They knew he was a praying person, but they also knew he got results. They saw the miracles he did, how the people were delivered or had demons cast out of them. Thank God. Jesus, the Word, and the Holy Ghost, that's God's will for us. God is truth, and he is not a man that would lie.

Isaiah 55:11 says that God's Word will not return void. Heaven and Earth may pass away, but not one jot or tittle of God's Word will pass away. The Word of the Lord is forever. No matter what critics do or say, they cannot change God's word. The Word of God will be forever.

Scripture References
Jeremiah 1:8
Jeremiah 1:17
Jeremiah 1:5
Proverbs 28:1
Romans 8:26
Numbers 23:19
Luke 11:1-13
Jeremiah 23:29
Matthew 5:18

The Word of God is like a hammer according to Jeremiah 23:29. The Holy Ghost spoke through Apostle Paul. I would like men to pray everywhere, lifting holy hands without wrath or doubt. When we lift our hands to the Lord, we should raise our hands in faith to the Lord. Lifting the hand is not only surrendering to the Lord but also praising the Lord. God has so much in store for his people. But we must see the force of the Lord. We must learn to fight on the offense rather than on the defense. We must learn to be sensitive to the voice of the Lord more than at any time in our lives. Because the enemy is working and plotting against the church, take care that we are not caught unaware of the wicked devices of the enemy.

God has promised that He would not leave us ignorant of Satan's devices. Therefore, we must get into the word and seek the Lord like never before. We must seek the face of the Lord because we will have to hear the voice of the Lord to receive instruction and direction from Him. In some situations, it could be life and death for us or our family, property, or wealth. All true prophets are intercessors, but all intercessors are not prophets. Just because a person spoke, a prophecy does not make them a prophet or prophetess. God is going to require more of us on the last day.

We must pray that we are counted worthy to escape these things that would come upon the Earth. There will be more people praying like never seen in our time. I remember that I said that in a meeting that I attended. There I saw a lot of people praying. I trust that it is not because of something serious or detrimental. But I strongly sense that it will be for that very reason. We need a prayer revival like never before.

That's a fantastic place to walk in the Lord or experience. We are seated in a heavenly place in Christ Jesus, above principalities, powers and dominion. Jesus is the High Priest and confession of our faith, a priest after the order of Melchizedek; Jesus is forever making intercessions for us. God is faithful. He is a faithful high priest. So think it not strange when those fiery trials come upon you, for it is trying of your faith working patience. Some of you need patience. For after that, then comes promise.

King David said, if I hide iniquity in my heart, the Lord will not hear me. God said in his word, "that which is not of faith is sin." God tells us faith worketh by love. Love is a weapon against the enemy. Remember the Apostle John. The Apostle John was full of the love of God, so when they tried to kill John by putting him into boiling oil. He did not die, so they put him on the Isle of Patmos and banished him with wild animals. But John was an influential disciple whom Jesus loved. On the Isle of Patmos, John was in the spirit on the Lord's day, and there John wrote the book of Revelations. God said, blessed is he who reads that book. We must contend for the faith that was once given among the Saints.

The Kingdom of God suffers violence, and the violent taketh by force. Satan has already been judged. Therefore, we fight from victory to victory, and success is ours.

> *Scripture References*
> *1 Corinthians 2:11*
> *2 Corinthians 7:14*
> *Luke 21:3,36*
> *Ephesians 2:6*
> *Ephesians 1:3*
> *1 Peter 4:12-19*
> *Hebrews 6:20*
> *Hebrews 7:1-21*
> *James 1:2-3*
> *Hebrews 5:6-10*
> *Hebrews 6:20*
> *Psalms 66:18*
> *Galatians 5:6*
> *Matthew 11:12*

"Nay, in all things we are more than conquerors."

Romans 8:37

"We have overcome this world for greater is he that is in us."

1 John 4:4

We have authority over the enemy. We have the Gospel of Jesus Christ. He is alive; he is not dead! God raised him from the dead. He is not in the grave; nobody got up out of that grave and is seated on the right hand of the Father, and He is coming back again. He was born on time, died on time, got out of the grave on time, and returned to the Father on time. He is coming back on time. Amen. I pray that we are ready. When He returns, if He doesn't come back and we are alive, I pray that we are counted worthy to escape those that would come upon the Earth. Evil will wax worse and worse, as in the days of Noah. God is a man of war. The battle is the Lords. Arise, O' Lord, and let your enemies be scattered.

In Deuteronomy Chapter 28, God said our enemy would come in one way and flee seven ways. Praise God for his Word. His word will never return void.

We must take the word and do warfare. We must also do warfare with the Lord's prophecy over our lives. Some of us have prophecies yet to be fulfilled in our lives. We must do warfare over those prophecies because the enemy will fight you to keep prophecies from coming to pass. But we must endure hardness like good soldiers. We must pray that God sends laborers, for the fields are ripe and ready to harvest. The fields are perishing. We must go into the byways and highways and compel them to come to the house or Kingdom of God. We must pray for God to send laborers into the harvest, for the fields are ripe and ready to harvest. If we pray, we can turn some things around. We can cancel or stop something the enemy has planned over our lives, against others, and over countries. God is a powerful God; He is a great and mighty God.

Scripture References
Exodus 15:3
Isaiah 55:11
Luke 21:25-36
Psalms 68:1
2 Timothy 3:13
Deuteronomy 28:7
2 Timothy 2:3-5
Luke 4:23
Matthew 9:38
Luke 10:2

With God, all things are possible when we believe according to Mark 9:23. First, we must know who we are in Christ, the power, and God's authority.

I trust the Lord that more churches will begin to pray more and have shut-in services. I pray that the ministers come and lay in sackcloth and ashes all night, that they would blow the trumpet and sound the alarm. I know that some of you will have divine appointments and revelations as we pray and seek the Lord. Elijah was a man of like passion just as we are. But Elijah prayed that it would not rain for three and a half years, and it did not rain for those years. He prayed again, and it rained as he prayed to the Lord, and the Lord answered. He sent out his servant, who saw a cloud about the size of a man's hand. Then it rained.

Elijah told his servant to say to King Ahab it would rain. Elijah outran the chariot that Ahab was riding. Elijah was a praying man and had power with God. Some of us will get into praying when deep calleth unto deep. You are going to find yourself talking spirit to Spirit.

That's a powerful thing to experience in God. There is a place in God where you will find yourself unable to say anything when you get into a level of worship or prayer. I remember I went into a level of worship, and all I could say was, Father. I could not say anything else at all. God is real and faithful. I have also talked with others, where we spoke spirit to spirit. One spirit man was talking to another. We should pray the same prayer that Jesus prayed; we would be one, even as the Father and I are one; we would be one with the body and one with Christ. He is the head, and we are the body. Amen.

> *"Put on the whole armor of God that you may be able to stand against all the wilds of the devil. Put on the helmet of salvation, the breastplate of righteousness. Your loins girt about with truth. Your feet shod with the gospel of preparing the gospel of peace. Take the shield of faith whenever ye can withstand all the fiery darts of the wicked one."*
>
> *Ephesians 6:10*

God told Abraham He was his shield and an exceedingly great reward. So extraordinary is our God. God made Abraham very rich and made a covenant with him. But the covenant that we have with Jesus is better. God is not a man who should lie; He cannot lie. God will not break the covenant. We may break the covenant, but not God.

> *Scripture References*
> *Numbers 23:19*
> *Joel 2:1*
> *Matthew 11:21*
> *John 17:21*
> *Colossian 1:18*
> *Genesis 15:1*
> *Genesis 13:2*
> *Genesis 17*
> *Psalms 89:34*

God said in Psalms: On the day of thy power, the people will be willing. When the glory of the Lord increases in the church, we will see glorious miracles. We will see the manifestation of the gifts restored. Jesus said He would not return until He made His enemies His footstool. God is doing great things this hour, but He will still do more incredible things. The level of glory the Lord wants to pour out on the church must be ready, or the church cannot handle or carry it. I know that when the glory of the Lord was so heavy upon me, I thought I would die. But Jesus prepared the church for what He had for it, but everybody will not be ready for what God will do. But a remnant of them is prepared for it. God is building His army. It will be a great army, and He will have people in different ranks. Some will try to break rank, but this will not work.

God will set back in order with the leadership of his kingdom—the apostle and prophet. There is a pattern to the church, just like God gave Moses how to build the tabernacle in the wilderness. God gave Moses specific orders and directions on how to build the tabernacle. The devil's kingdom has ranking spirits and demons as well. Satan will never win. Read the back of the book we win. We must endure hardness as good soldiers. God will fight with His army to win this last and great battle for souls. I believe angels will accompany those specifically about our Father's business and the winning of souls. We should expect miracles and the supernatural. Jesus is a forever high priest after the order of Melchizedek.

Abraham paid tithes to Melchizedek. Abraham paid tithes before tithing was introduced to the children of Israel. Abraham was a man that sought the Lord; he was a friend of God. He defeated the enemy when it was time to defend himself and his family. Abraham had trained some men for battle. God himself also is building himself an army. Joel says this army will not break rank. God is moving by His spirit. As I write this book, miracles, signs, and wonders will occur.

God is calling the church to mature and come into the full stature of Christ. I believe that God is going to do a quick work. I believe that God will call the church to a deeper walk with Him, and it will be through His Word and prayer. The early church was powerful. They went from house to house breaking bread. They were in the Word, and they prayed. I believe the church will also be gathering in the home again. The Bible talks about the church in the houses.

As I said earlier, many of us will receive instruction and direction from the Lord in prayer. God will also bring the apostles, prophets, and many others who have been hindered or stopped. Some of these ministers and people will be placed on the front line. God will fight alongside His church. The angels will fight alongside ministers in prayer. Churches are going to spring up all over the world. The church will catch the revelation and contend for the faith given among the saints.

Eyes have not seen, nor ears have heard God's things in store for them. I also believe great persecution will come to the church. If we were praying and, in the Word, we would be ready and able to stand; having done all, we will stand. I also believe those who will not obey God will walk away from ministry. Some will fall to such depths that they will be shut down and not want to repent and make the right choices or change. There will be great deliverance. I also know there is a realm of glory that the enemy will not be able to hide but will be manifested and exposed. There are levels in the realm of glory. You can get to a level of glory that will bring fear. There is also a level of glory you can get into, and you will think you will die if it continues because it is so strong upon you. I have personally experienced these levels of glory. It is not something you can forget. Some of us have lost much. Some have left much to follow Jesus.

Mark 10:29 is a scripture that is just on restoration. God will restore all that the enemy has taken. Satan will not want you to get it back, but God will restore all the thief has taken. Everything you lost will be restored. When the thief has been caught, He shall restore sevenfold. Believe the Lord; let every man be a liar and only God be true. I know that something is stirring in the realm of the Spirit. The gifts will be restored to the church again in a powerful way. The gift of the Spirit is a part of our weaponry.

> *Scripture References*
> *Psalms 110:3*
> *Hebrews 4:14*
> *Joel 2:7*
> *Acts 1:13*
> *Jude 1:3*
> *Proverbs 6:31*
> *Romans 3:4*

We need not worry. We can cast all our cares on the Lord, for we know He cares for us. We are going to have more divine encounters with the Lord. We will also have more divine appointments with people. Beware of how we trust everybody; some may interact with angels unaware. To God be the glory for everything He has done and is doing. God may tell some of us to be still and know I am God. Remember, in Isaiah 42:13, God is a man of war. The battle is the Lord's, and He does not lose any battles. Remember, keep the faith; we win.

Don't give up on your dreams. Dream big. As we pray, we can cancel or stop things in the Spirit that the enemy has tried to do. We have authority and power given to us by Jesus. We must walk in our purpose. We must take God at His Word and say, if God said it, that it's it. Let every man be a liar, and only God be true.

"We shall know the truth, and the truth shall make us free."

John 8:32

"I am the way, the truth, and the life. No man can come to the Father except by me."

John 14:6

The Word of God will never return void. Heaven and earth shall pass away, but not one jot or tittle of God's Word will pass away. Heaven and earth will pass away, but not God's Word. God's truth will always prevail. The Word of God is powerful. Jesus defeated the devil with the Word in the wilderness. In Matthew 4:1-11 chapter, whenever the devil tempted Jesus, Jesus always said, "it is written." He overcame the devil.

Spiritual warfare is high. Even as I write these words, the enemy is plotting and planning. We are not ignorant of Satan's devices. I have always said we should know our enemy, prayer warriors, and intercessors. I encourage you to get on your watch because when you spend time with the Lord, he will reveal some things to you. Just like God uses people, the devil uses people. Obey the Lord.

> *Scripture References*
> *1 Peter 5:7*
> *Psalms 55:22*
> *Psalms 46:10*
> *Exodus 15:3*
> *2 Chronicles 20:15*
> *Romans 3:4*
> *Isaiah 55:11*
> *Matthew 5:18*
> *2 Corinthians 12:11*

Isaiah 1:18-19 says if ye are willing and obedient, ye shall eat the good of the land, but ye shall be devoured of it if ye rebel. While journaling in the presence of God, I know that spiritual warfare is going on like never before. But God has His angels in place, and they are doing warfare with the evil spirits of this age. We should be fighters on the offense rather than the defense. Many things will happen that are prophesied in God's Word. The spirit of the antichrist is stronger than it has ever been before. I spent much time in prayer, and on October 22, 2003, I was awakened with laughter.

I was so happy, and I felt great. I knew that it was the doing of the Lord. I had not laughed in the Spirit like that in a while. I have laughed so much throughout the years that they have had to carry me to my car. I was praising God for changing my life and taking me to another level in Him. I was never the same after that encounter with the Lord in my sleep. I know that God is restoring something to me. God is also restoring something to the church. You will probably hear me talk about restoration a lot because that is so strong in my spirit. Great things are happening right now, even as the Holy Spirit gives me what to write in this book. Eyes have not seen, nor ears heard, God's things for those of us who love Him. But God hath revealed them unto us by his Spirit: for the Spirit searcheth all things, yea, the deep things of God. God is going to deal with our hearts and bring conviction upon us. God said in his Word that He would cleanse the filth of the daughters of Zion with burning and purging.

God will sanctify the church. We will walk in the Spirit to not fulfill the lust of the flesh. Some evil spirits have been released into the earth. There are strong spirits of seduction, lust, and unclean spirits. We will have to get closer to God through the Word and prayer. God is going to anoint the church with fresh oil. We will walk into a new level of anointing. The church is transitioning. Some people will shift, but God has been trying to transition the church, but the leaders are unwilling to take the people to a higher level. There will be a remnant that will go there, but we will go there. Will you be one of the ones that will say yes to God? God is raising an army that builds His kingdom and tears the devil's kingdom down. Let no man deceive you. God is calling His people to believe and to walk in His righteousness. There is power and authority in the name of Jesus. The blood of Jesus and the Word of the Lord God has given us everything we need to overcome the enemy and work and live victorious lives in this wicked and perverse generation. God is with us. He is Jehovah Shamma, Emmanuel – God with us.

"Thou shalt also decree a thing, and it shall be established unto thee: and the light shall shine upon thy ways."

Job 22:28

Many of us will declare and decree something, and it will happen. Some of you have already been declaring and decreeing something. Continue to declare and decree in faith, and the Lord will answer. The prayers of a righteous man availeth much. God will do great things in this hour for His church. We are getting ready to see God move like never before. No matter what happens, we are more than conquerors through Christ, that loves us.

We are more than conquerors through Him that loves us. God is calling for the church to mature so that we can receive the meat of the Word of God. God wants to restore some things to the church, but they are not ready to receive them. But God will have a remnant that is going to receive it. Walk in it, obey, and accept it. We are going to know God in very different and new ways. God is a God of the covenant. He will not break the covenant. We may break the covenant, but not God, for God is faithful to the faithful.

Behold, I have given you the power to tread upon serpents and scorpions and over the enemy's strength. Deep calleth into deep. We are getting ready to walk into the more profound things of God. Deep revelations. God said He would not do anything on the earth until He first revealed it to His servants, the prophets.

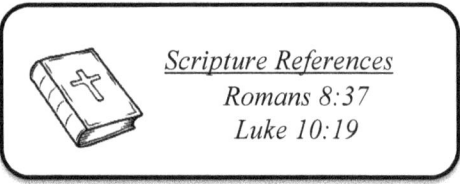

Scripture References
Romans 8:37
Luke 10:19

God is revealing things to his servants, the Prophets, and the Prophets will speak. They speak the Word of the Lord. Many will speak what God is saying to the church in this hour. Some will tell what is happening in the Spirit realm. Some God will use to confirm, exhort or encourage. Some will root up, tear down or pluck up and rebuild. Some doctrines need to be rooted out of the church, then replaced with true doctrine or revelation of truth.

God talks about false prophets and false teachers these last days. There are many false prophets and teachers. Jesus said you know those that say they are apostles and are not. Jesus has said that in his word. We will have to discern which is good and which is evil. We are going to need gifts like never before. The gifts are our weapons. Satan's power is no match for the power of God. God talks about principalities, powers, and dominion. But God has given Jesus all power, and He has shown that power and dominion over all the enemy's power. Let's rise and take over our place in the dominion of God. Let's rise and take back everything the devil has stolen, hindered, or stopped in our lives. Paul said in Galatians to the Galatians, you did run, but who hindered you? Take your dream back, family, vision, finances, families, strength, whatever the devil has stolen. Remember, we won! The victory is ours.

> *Scripture References*
> *Isaiah 4:4*
> *1 Corinthians 2:9-10*
> *Galatians 5:16*
> *Isaiah 7:14*
> *Ezekiel 48:35*
> *James 5:16*
> *Psalms 89:34*
> *Deuteronomy 7:9*
> *Psalms 42:7*
> *Amos 3:7*
> *Jeremiah 1:16*
> *Jeremiah 31:28*
> *Galatians 5:7*
> *Revelations 2:2*
> *Matthew 7:15*

One day, the Lord said, "If you don't quit, you will win." I believe God. When we start in faith, we must finish in faith. People say when God gives you something, the devil can't take, or you won't lose it. That is a false doctrine. God blessed Job, and the devil stole everything he had. Had God not told him that he could not touch his life after he removed the hedge round about him? God had other plans for Job to fulfill, but the devil would have taken his life. Satan is a thief, a murderer, a destroyer. But Job, like many of us, when the test is so severe, we don't fully understand what is going on, so sometimes we say things that are not true.

Job said that which I had greatly feared has come upon me. Well, Job thought that what he feared would come upon him was why he was going through what he was going through with losing his children and livestock. But that was not the reason why Job lost all that he had. Satan is an accuser of thy brethren. God himself asked Satan if he had tried his faithful servant Job, who walked upright before him and was perfect. Satan said he served you because he was the wealthiest man in the land and had so much. But it was a lie. After the Lord removed the hedge, the devil put forth his hand and touched Job. He had sores or boils from the top of his head to the sole of his feet. God knew He could trust Job. Job did not doubt God, even when his wife saw him suffering. She told him to curse God and die.

Scripture References
John 18:12
John 2:23
Job 1:8
Job 3:25
Job 2:7,9-13
Job 2:3
Matthew 24:13
Job 42:10
Hebrews 10:36
Ephesians 2:16
Hebrews 6:12
2 Timothy 3:12
James 1:3-4

Job said, "woman, you sound foolish. I am going to wait for my appointed time." Job knew that his change would come. He knew he would come forth as pure gold. It was not because of what Job said that was why he was going through what he was going through, but he was tried and tested.

Satan was going to and fro before with the sons of God. God could not trust everybody with that type of test or trial. Many would fail the test, but Job trusted God until the end. Those that endure until the end shall be saved. But we won!

But Job forgave his friends that had come against him during the test or trial. God restored Job double for all that he had lost. He even had more children. His daughters were the most beautiful in the land. God is awesome. It's not always because you are doing something wrong, but you may trust because you are doing the right things. All that live godly in Christ Jesus shall suffer persecution. The trying of your faith worketh patience.

After patience, then comes the promise. Let patience have her perfect work. You will want nothing. We are complete with Him. I have heard teachings about Job. They have thought he went through what he went through because he said that with him, fear had significantly come upon him. But it is an erroneous doctrine or teaching about Job. But Job's test was different. The devil is a liar. He wanted Job to fail God, but he did not forget God. Job was faithful until the end. He stood the test of time and came out victorious and more blessed when he came out of the severe tests and trials than when he went in. God blessed him double in everything he lost. Hallelujah!! Glory to God! God knows all!

Not even the gates of hell will or have been able to prevail against the church. The church is a powerful kingdom. The Kingdom of God is the most powerful if we know who we are. God will reveal even more truth unto us by His spirit.

"We shall know the truth, and the truth shall make us free."

John 8:32

"He waits upon the Lord shall renew his strength; they shall mount up with wings as an eagle; run and not be weary; walk and not faint."

Isaiah 40:31

When you spend time in God's presence in the Word, praise, and worship, you will find that your strength is renewed. You will be able to run the race with the power of the Lord. You will look like you haven't been through anything. Like the three Hebrew boys, Shadrach, Meshach, and Abednego, there was no smell of smoke on them. People have often told me that I look younger and more beautiful. I cannot take any credit or glory for this. To God be all the glory, honor, and praise. At this time, I was going through one of the most significant tests of my life and temptation from the enemy, a great spiritual battle, but I won.

My life is in God's hands. My Father loves me and has great things in store for me and a great plan. His will be done, and His kingdom will come in my life. The plan that God has will be manifested to the minute detail. God predestined us before the foundation of the world, but the enemy will not let God's plan for our life be manifested that easily. But we can work with God to bring to pass and fulfill our planned purpose and destiny. God's will be done, His kingdom come. The Kingdom of God is within us. I expect God's plan to be manifested in my life and family to the minute detail. If necessary, God will make a way where there seems to be no way. God has all power in His hands. He has given us the authority we need to live a victorious life. I expect God to do the impossible because everything is possible when we believe in Him. God will give us the strength and grace we need. His grace is sufficient.

> *Scripture References*
> *Job 42:10-15*
> *Matthew 16:18*
> *1 Corinthians 2:10*
> *Daniel 3:8-25*
> *Matthew 6:9-13*
> *Mark 9:23*
> *Luke 17:21*
> *Romans 1:4*

When Paul received the revelation from God, he was given a thorn in his flesh, a messenger of Satan, to buffet him. He had tests and trials everywhere he went. God told Ananias to go and tell Paul what he would suffer for his namesake. God instructed Paul about where he would take the gospel and places he should not go at that season and time. God told Paul that he would need to go before Caesar in Rome. Paul knew exactly where he needed to go. God is faithful. He will fulfill His Word in our lives to minute detail. But Paul told Timothy that he had to take the prophecy given to him by the presbytery and do warfare over them. Sometimes, we have to do warfare over the prophetic words sent to us by God. It is not flesh and blood that we are fighting but powers and principalities and spiritual wickedness in high places.

When the prophet Daniel had prayed and fasted, the prince of Persia held up the Angel Gabriel, a messenger, from bringing the prayer through. But God sent Michael, the archangel, to get the prayer through. They put Daniel in the lion's den because he would not stop praying to God or obeying the command of the King. But God told Daniel that from the very first day, he set himself to seek the face of the Lord. The answer was on the way, but the Prince of Persia held up Gabriel, the messenger angel. Sometimes, there is a battle in the realm of the spirit, and we are unaware of why our answer has not come through. But we must be persistent and persevere and not give up, knowing that the answer will come through. Remember, God is fighting for us, and Jesus is interceding for us. Sometimes, you may hear the Holy Spirit say the battle is the Lord's.

Let's remember that God does not lose battles; He always wins. Remember, it is Him that endures until the end; He shall be saved. Remember, we win!!

Our prayers should be based on the Word of God. We should always put God's Word first and make God's Word a priority in our lives. When we put God's Word first in our lives, we base our lives on the truth because God's Word is truth. John 8:32: Ye shall know the truth, and the truth shall make you free, for we are washed by the washing of the water of the word. The Word of the Lord will cleanse us. Through the blood of Jesus, He washes us daily and cleanses us from all unrighteousness.

According to Hebrews 4:12, the Word of God is powerful and sharper than any two-edged sword. It pierces the heart's content and is a discerner of thought, even to the marrow of the bone. God has given us everything that we need to live an overcoming life.

"Nay, in all things, we are more than conquerors."

Romans 8:37

We need to trust God for the answers in our life. For it's the anointing that destroys the yokes. We must confess the Word in faith. Jesus said we have what we say. So that should encourage us to acknowledge or speak God's Word more.

> *Scripture References*
> *1 Corinthians 12:9*
> *2 Corinthians 12:6-7*
> *Daniel 11:16-33*
> *Acts 9:16*
> *Acts 2:24-27*
> *1 Timothy 1:18*
> *2 Corinthians 6:7*
> *Daniel 10:13-14*
> *Ephesians 6:12*
> *2 Chronicles 20:15*
> *Daniel 10:13*
> *Romans 8:31*
> *1 John 1:7-9*
> *Ephesians 5:26*
> *1 John 1:7-19*
> *Isaiah 10:27*
> *Mark 11:23-24*

Sometimes, we have to say and say it. Sometimes, we have to say it over and over and over. But, we have to say it and say it until it gets down in our hearts until our faith has increased.

Faith cometh by hearing and hearing by the Word of God according to Romans 10:17. For out of the abundance of the heart, the mouth speaks. Let's not let our words be stout against God. God said that not having faith is a sin. If we don't walk in faith, we sin against God. The just shall walk by faith and not by sight.

The just shall live by faith. We must speak the Word of God repeatedly and do it in faith. Faith comes by hearing and hearing the Word of God. We must get a desire to listen to the Word of the Lord. By our words, we are condemned, or by our words, we are justified.

Therefore, now there is no condemnation to those who walk in the spirit and not after the flesh according to Romans 8:1. God is faithful to his Word, and he does not change.

"Jesus Christ, the same yesterday, today, and forever."

Hebrews 13:8

We are in spiritual warfare like never before. We must keep our armor on and God's Word in our hearts. Remember to praise and worship the Lord. David said I meditate in thy Word.

Joshua said, thou shall meditate upon the Word both day and night, then shalt thou make thy way prosperous, and thou shall have success.

We must grow up and mature in the things of God. We know it's alright to start on the milk of the Word of God but must go on to eat the meat of the Word. Indeed, we should desire the sincere milk of the Word so we may grow. A good man, out of the treasures of his heart, brings forth good things. Out of the abundance of the heart, an evil man brings forth evil, for the mouth speaks out of the abundance of the heart. We must say what God has said, or His Word has said. When we start automatically speaking the Word of God over Christians or situations, we know that the Word of God is in our hearts. We will go through tests and trials, sometimes even fiery ones. But we continue in faith. Stand upon God's Word in faith, and God will bring us through victoriously. For it is always God who leads us to triumph in Christ Jesus. We won!! God will bring us through, take us through, and bring us through.

> *Scripture References*
> *Habakkuk 2:4*
> *Romans 14:23*
> *Matthew 12:37*
> *Joshua 1:8*
> *1 Peter 2:2*
> *Matthew 12:34-35*
> *Luke 6:45*

Hebrews 11:6 says he that comes to God must believe that he is and that he is a rewarder of them that diligently seek him. When diligently seeking God, we must believe that we have the petition or desire that we have sought God for. 1 John 5:14 says this is the confidence that we have if we ask anything according to His will; He heareth us. If He heareth us, we have the petitions that we ask of Him.

We must believe and trust that God will answer our prayers, for God is still in the miracle and supernatural business. He has not changed.

He is the same yesterday, today, and forever says Hebrews 13:8. God is moving, but we haven't seen anything yet. We are getting ready to see God do something that we have never seen before in our lives. We will see creative miracles, God's supernatural power, and the Lord's glory. In that place or glory of the Lord, you can think thoughts, and it happens.

There is also a place in God where the glory of God can be so powerful that you think you are going to die. I have experienced all these things in God and fully concur with what I experienced. God wants the latter-day church to walk in. I believe the early church, the book of Acts church, touched its beginning. But Jesus said I will not return until the restitution of all things. God is a God of miracles. He is doing the impossible. Even as I write this book, I am blessed, even though I have been in an extraordinary attack by the enemy. But I have the victory! If we suffer with Him, we shall reign with Him. God said, "All that live godly in Christ Jesus will suffer persecution." The blessing of the Lord maketh us rich and addeth no sorrow with it. God has pleasure in the prosperity of His servant.

The areas the devil fights the church more than anything else are their funds and health. God said, above all things, I wish that thou mayest prosper and be in health, even as thy soul prospers. In Acts 10:38, God anointed Jesus of Nazareth, who went about doing good and healing all oppressed by the devil, for God was with him. God is with us. If God is for us, who can be against us? God is Jehovah Shamma, the God that is with us. He is Emanuel, God with us, and He will never leave us. He will be with us until the end of the ages. Therefore, we should not be afraid or discouraged.

"For God has not given us a spirit of fear but power, love, and a sound mind."

2 Timothy 1:7

The Lord said the righteous are as bold as a lion. We are righteous in Christ; we are complete in Christ. God will perfect those things that concern us. Therefore, we must keep our armor on.

Read and meditate on Ephesians 6—Never go to battle against the enemy without our armor. We must fight the good fight of faith. We must keep ourselves covered in the blood of Jesus. We know who we are in Christ Jesus. There is power in the blood of Jesus. We are not fighting against flesh and blood but powers, principalities and dominions, and spiritual wickedness in high places. We are not fighting against flesh and blood, for the enemy has come down with great wrath, for he knows that his time is short. Jesus said, "Woe unto the inhabitants of the earth." Jesus has already defeated the enemy, so He has given us that same power and authority to defeat the enemy. Don't back up from the enemy; press forward. Enforce his defeat with the Word of God, the blood of Jesus, and the armor of God. Put on, Christ. By all means, use the name of Jesus. Jesus said, whatever we ask the Father in his name, Jesus' name, He will do it. Jesus said, more wondrous works than these shall we do because I go to my Father. Jesus has already been glorified. So He has already sent the Holy Ghost, our helper, our comforter, counselor, our power.

Scripture References
1 Timothy 6:12
John 14:12
John 6:63
Revelation 12:12
Psalms 138:8
Proverbs 28:1
Romans 8:31
Act 3:21
2 Timothy 2:2
Proverbs 10:22
2 Timothy 3:12
Psalms 35:27
3 John 2

According to Acts 1:8, Ye shall receive power. After that, the Holy Ghost will come upon you. Over thirty years ago, when I used to have prayer and Bible study in my home, and we went house to house on Wednesdays and Tuesdays, I said to the saints if we had the same Holy Ghost that the saints had on the day of Pentecost, and the saints were before the early church. Then we should be doing the work and more excellent work. Jesus will not return until the restitution of all things. Jesus is coming back for a powerful church, a church that is walking in His authority and power, a glorious church. A church without a spot or wrinkle or blemish. God is sanctifying His church.

Indeed, we will be tested and tried. All that live godly in Christ Jesus will suffer persecution. Nevertheless, God is getting ready to show out and reveal his strength. We will be strong in the Lord and the power of His might.

For Psalms 110:3 says that the people will be willing on the day of thy power. It's God's set time to favor Zion. I thank God for the encounters and experiences I have experienced with Jesus, but there are more extraordinary powers and glory for me and others to share. Take the limit off of God and go to another realm in God.

Those realms and places in praise that you can go to. I remember, in prayer, I got into a realm of worship with God. All I could say was, Father, Father. I said it over and over, but nothing else would come out. There are not only levels of glory and levels of faith but also levels of prayer that you can get into. Deep calleth unto deep, David said in the Psalms. We must fight the good fight of faith like never before. If we don't quit, we win. Perfect love casts out all fear, for faith works by love. Paul said, examine yourself. See if you are in the faith. James said faith without works is dead. He said, show me your faith and I will show you my works. We must work out our soul salvation with fear and trembling.

God is raising a mighty army. I know that I saw a lot of people praying. I know that God will bring that vision to pass. I also know He will raise true apostles, prophets, and prophetesses.

The church is built upon the apostles and prophets. And Jesus Christ, who is the head cornerstone according to Ephesians 2:20. Call unto me, and I show thee great and mighty things that thou knowest not. God said the answer is on the way before you ask or while speaking. He told Daniel that the answer was on the way when he first set his heart to seek him with prayer and fasting. But the Prince of Persia held up the messenger angel, Gabriel, in the heavens. But Michael the archangel brought the angel through. I believe that God will allow the angels to get involved in our life more in these last days. Also, ministry spirits to those of us of our salvation.

Daniel did not stop praying; he kept praying and believing in God. Paul and Silas sought God, and the angels got involved. The angels released Peter from jail, and then he preached salvation to the jailers. Peter was put in prison after they killed James. They sought to kill Peter, but they had an all-night prayer meeting for Peter, and the angel came and released him from prison. We have to make a connection with God by faith. We must tap into or operate in the God of faith. We must work out of the spirit of faith.

While journaling these words, I have had quite a few people come to or call me for prayer, and God worked miracles, healings, and deliverances. To God be the glory. There will be so many people who will need miracles, whether they are miracles of healing, finances, family, or marriage. Even more, I believe that God will have people ready for the task of the kingdom to His kingdom business. The kingdom of God does rule. The heavens rule. Some people in God's kingdom will be ready and endure hardness as good soldiers.

If ye have run with footman and they have wearied you, how can ye endure in the swelling of the Jordan? God says that even minor tests or trials can disturb your peace. Then when things are tough, you will not be able to handle them.

God is Jehovah Rapha. Our healer. He is our strength, the strength of our life. Let the sick say I am healed; the poor say, I am rich; the weak say, I am strong. We must say what we want and desire from God.

According to Mark 11:22-24, have faith in God. For verily I say unto you, whosoever shall say unto the mountain, be thou removed and cast into the sea but doubt not in his heart he shall have whatsoever he saith. If we say it enough and get it into our hearts, we will have whatsoever we say. For out of the abundance of heart, the mouth speaks. For every idle word and deed that we speak, we will give account for it on judgment day. There is no distance in the realm of the spirit.

"He sent his Word and healed them."

Psalms 107:20

Jesus said about the Centurion that He had not seen such great faith in Israel. But with the women with the issue of blood for twelve years, said within herself, if she would touch the helm of His garment, she would be whole. And she was made whole. Jesus said go in peace, your faith has made you whole. She had spent all she had on physicians. Jesus was on His way to heal Jairus' daughter who was sick, but she died. Jesus raised her from the dead. It was the Centurion's servant that was sick as well. More wondrous works than these shall we do. Praise God. To God be the glory.

Scripture References
Ephesians 5:27
Ezekiel 48:35
Luke 5:27
Acts 3:21
2 Timothy 3:12
Ephesians 6:10
Philippians 2:12
James 2:14
Psalms 102:13
Psalms 42:7
1 John 4:18
Galatians 5:6
2 Corinthians 13:5
James 2:16-18
Jeremiah 3:33
Daniel 10:12
Acts 12:2-5
2 Kings 19:35
Luke 7:1-10
Luke 8:40-48
Mark 5:21-43

> *Scripture References*
> Mark 9:20-22
> Matthew 12:34-36
> Luke 6:45
> Matthew 9:20-22
> Ephesians 2:4-10
> Daniel 4:26
> Jeremiah 12:5
> Acts 12:8-17

I am expecting more incredible miracles to take place. I am expecting God to do the impossible. I take the limit off of God. We don't want to be like the children of Israel, who said, "Can God furnish a table in the wilderness?" Full of doubt and unbelief and doubt. Also, the man Elijah the prophet, gave the Word that by tomorrow, they would be able to buy flour for two shekels. But the man said if there be windows in heaven, he did not believe that was possible, full of doubt and unbelief. But the prophet told him that he would not see it. He was trampled on and killed. He did not experience miracles, so we must watch our words.

"Ye have overcome this world for greater is he that is in you than he that is in the world."

1 John 4:4

Psalms 89:34 says that God will not break the covenant, nor will He alter the words that have gone out His mouth. God is not a man that He should lie, nor the son of man that He should repent. Hath He spoke it, and shall He not make it good. He has said that God's Word will be forever; shall He not do it? I remember when I was growing up, there was a saying, sticks and stones may break my bones, but words will never hurt me. Over the year, I have learned that words are powerful, whether negative or positive. God says in His Word that death and life are in the power of your tongue, but they that love it shall eat the fruits thereof. God said I set before you life and death. Choose life. If we need a favor, we should ask God for the favor and believe that He will give us a blessing.

Proverbs 3:4 says that so shall you find favor and give understanding in the sight of God and man. Psalms 5:12: God will encompass us with a shield. God will be our exceeding great reward. God is faithful to his Word. He cannot lie, and He will not change. Not one jot or one tittle of His Word will pass.

Heaven and earth can pass away, but not God's Word. If we trust God, He will do exceedingly, abundantly above all we can ask or think, according to the power working in us.

"If I abide in you and my words abide in you, you can ask what you will, and it shall be done unto you."

John 15:7

We must abide in Him and Him in us, then we can ask the Father anything in His name and receive it. The kingdom of God does rule. The kingdom of God is within us.

"Whatsoever ye shall bind on with shall be bound in heaven. Whatsoever we lose on earth shall be released in the heavens."

Matthew 18:18

May God give all of us a greater revelation of His Word. May the Word of God become alive in our spirits. God is real, and He is alive. Jesus is alive. He is not dead; He is alive. He has risen. Praise the Lord, for his mercy endures forever. God does not change. Is anything too hard for God? With God, all things are possible when we believe. We must believe and trust in His Word. God is real. Psychologists, anthropologists, doctors, and others in the medical field are beginning to believe in God. Some have even started to believe that God is real and that Jesus is alive. Even demons are to admit to something about God. Jesus is alive. God will bless His people with peace.

Because when we know that we are righteous in Christ, we will have His peace. God's promises are yes and amen. God will not break the covenant, nor will He alter the words that have gone out of His mouth. Even as I am journaling these words, God makes Himself more real to me. Okay, but I want to know Him more and get closer to Him. By God's grace, I will draw closer to Him in prayer and the Word. God has said I will build my church upon this rock, and the gates of hell shall not prevail. We must seek the face of God like never before. God has given us many promises in His Word, so His Word will not return to Him void.

Isaiah 55:8 says for His thoughts are not our thoughts; neither His ways our ways, but His thoughts are higher than our thoughts, His ways higher than our ways. But God said in his Word that Israel knew the acts of God, but Moses knew the ways of God. How powerful is that? Moses knew the ways of God. I trust that God can say that about each of us. I hope that God can say that about each of us. God is faithful; He is merciful. He is good, and his mercy endureth forever. I trust that our ways please the Lord.

> *Scripture References*
> *Psalms 136:1*
> *Psalms 100:5*
> *Psalms 103: 7*
> *Isaiah 55:11*
> *Matthew 16:18*
> *Psalms 89:34*
> *2 Corinthians 1:20*
> *Genesis 18:14*
> *1 Chronicles 16:34*
> *Psalms 136:10*
> *Mark 9:23*
> *Matthew 28:6*
> *Jeremiah 32:27*
> *John 14:13, 16-23*
> *Matthew 5:18*
> *Ephesians 3:20*
> *Psalms 5:12*
> *Genesis 15:1*
> *Numbers 23:19*
> *Proverbs 18:21*
> *Psalms 78:19-22*
> *2 Kings 7:19*

I know that God has said evil would wax worse and worse. But God has said that we should pray to escape the things that would come upon the earth. Spiritual warfare has increased and will increase more. But I also know that God will hide us in His pavilion until all these things are passed over. There is a secret place that we can hide in and trust the Lord. He is Jehovah Nissi, Jehovah Shalom—our peace, sword, and shield. God is our shield and sword. How great is our God? God has said in His Word that eyes have not seen, nor ears heard, the things God has in store for them that love Him. God hath revealed them to us by His Spirit.

Satan is the God of this world, but God owns it all. God can do anything but fail. We are in spiritual warfare like never before. Some don't want to face the fact that we are in a spiritual battle, but if we wish to admit it, we are still in a war of good and evil. The warfare will increase not decrease. We cannot get comfortable when things are going well. We must continue to confess the Word in faith. God spoke everything into this world. He made man from the dust of the earth. He put Adam asleep, took a rib from Adam's side, and made Eve. What a mighty God that we serve. He is all-knowing, all-powerful. He is the best thing that could ever happen to us—no matter the test or trial we go through. God will always be with us. No matter what we go through, God will bring us to victory. God will not let us down. He will get us through every time.

> *Scripture References*
> *Luke 21:36*
> *2 Timothy 3:13*
> *Psalms 27:5*
> *1 Corinthians 2:9-10*
> *2 Corinthians 4:4*
> *Genesis 2:22*

Spiritual warfare is so great, and it will get even more intense. That is why we must be on our guard night and day. Your spirit is real, and He knows all things. He is alive, and the spirit world is as real as the natural world. God spoke the world into existence. We must realize we are not fighting flesh and blood but powers and principalities. As I journal these words, I know the enemy is plotting against the church. Therefore, we must watch what we say and do. We must follow the instruction and direction of the Holy Spirit like never before. It is going to require that we spend more time with the Lord. Also, we must have more extraordinary revelations of God, who we are in Christ, who our enemy is, and what he is plotting. God said He would not leave us ignorant of Satan's devices. We must be as wise as a serpent but as harmless as a dove. God will not leave us ignorant of Satan's devices. God will not allow us to be tempted above what we can bear. But will make a way to escape.

Scripture References
Matthew 10:16
1 Corinthians 10:13
Ephesians 6:12
2 Corinthians 2:11

We will see and hear of more angelic activity in these last days. The angels will often help us when we get ready to work for the Lord or accompany us in our everyday affairs. God is a man of war. He is faithful, and He cannot lie. What God has spoken in his Word, He will do. God is going to show Himself strong. There are giants in the realm of the spirit. But giants do fall and will fall. When the enemy comes in like a flood, the spirit of the Lord will lift a standard against our enemies. I know the enemy has his army together and will continue to do so. But he has an end. God is building his army. Will you be a significant part of his army? Will you say yes? We are getting ready to see some of the greatest miracles we have ever seen. Jesus spoke more wondrous works than these shall we do than He did. God has given a commission to the church as a whole. God also has a pattern for the church. I must pray and seek the Lord. The early church touches the beginning of it during their time.

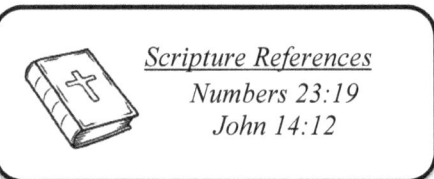

Scripture References
Numbers 23:19
John 14:12

The apostles, prophets, and church turned the known world upside down with the gospel. Paul finished his course with joy and fought the good fight of faith. Prepare yourself in the Word and prayer. Surround yourself with the Word of God's prayer. We must speak the Word in prayer and faith.

> *Scripture References*
> *Acts 2:20-24*
> *Act 17:6*
> *John 13:1*
> *Acts 20:24*

Everything we do must be done in faith. Paul said to examine yourself to see whether you are in the faith. Jesus said when I come, will I find faith in the earth? We will have discernment like never before and the gifts of the spirit. Stir up the gifts of God in you. For the Holy Ghost gives gifts to whom He will. Just remember, we win!

We must pray that God will send laborers into the harvest. The harvest is plentiful, but the laborers are few. For the fields are white and ready to harvest. For the harvest is perishing, people are dying and stepping into eternity. Many are young, and some are old and full of age. So let's get serious about God's blessings. I minister to a lot of people. I have seen many miracles of healing, deliverance, and salvation. Sometimes, people need a word of encouragement. But we must be instant in season and out of season. One will put a thousand to flight, and two will put ten thousand. It is a powerful thing for the church to agree.

Jesus said in St. John the 17th chapter that they might be one even as Father and I are one. So God spoke through his servant David in Psalms, as the dew ran upon Mount Herman, so the anointing ran down Aaron's beard and the oil. There God will command a blessing. I have been so blessed writing this book, as the Holy Spirit has given me the words to put to pen.

> *Scripture References*
> 2 Corinthians 12:11
> Luke 18:8
> Matthew 9:38
> Luke 10:2
> Joshua 23:10
> 2 Timothy 2:14
> Psalms 133:1-3
> Deuteronomy 32:30
> 2 Timothy 4:2
> Joshua 23:10
> 2 Timothy 4:2
> Matthew 9:38
> Luke 10:2

Praise the Lord for his goodness. You will see the church go from strength to strength, faith to faith, glory to glory, and victory to victory. As I write this book, I sense something so incredible that God is getting to do.

According to Amos 3:7, God said He would do nothing on the earth unless revealing first them to His servants, the prophets. To God be all glory, praise, and honor for His Word. It's almost as if the apostles and prophets are in hiding. But God will bring them forth into the earth. There will be a revival that the world has never seen. The glory of the Lord will bring healing, blessing, and deliverance upon the people like never before. We are getting ready to see some of the more wondrous works, creative miracles, and the supernatural power of God move like never before. God will restore all things. Many are going to return to prayer and fasting with dedication. The enemy will hate that because he knows it gives you more sensitivity and power with God.

We need to seek God and the scriptures like never before, truly living in the Word. For the Word that Jesus speaks, they are spirit and life.

The Apostles would not leave the Word and prayer to wait on tables or help the Grecian woman complaining. We must guard our hearts with all diligence, for out it flows the issues of life. We should not let the Word of God depart from our eyes. We should meditate upon the Word, day and night, and then we shall prosper. We must submit ourselves to God and resist the devil, and he will flee. We need the anointing in our lives like never before. There is a rest unto the children of God. The children of Israel did not enter into the rest of the Lord because of their unbelief. I cannot emphasize enough that our spirituality has gotten greater.

> *Scripture References*
> *Job 22:28*
> *Acts 6:4*
> *Proverbs 4:20-27*
> *James 4:7*
> *Joshua 1:8*
> *Hebrews 3:19*

We are in dangerous times. Evil is getting worse and worse. It will certainly not get any better, so we should put our army boots on in the spirit and get used to hardness as good soldiers. We should get in the trenches and fight to win. We are winners. If it had not been for the Lord on our side, we would not have made it this far. But if God is for us, who can be against us? We must know these things to win! Who we are and what Jesus is in us. We must understand that the battle is already won. We fight from victory to victory. The devil is already defeated. He already is judged. God has given us everything that we need to fight and win. We are winners. The back of the book tells us that we win. I believe in God. God cannot lie. The devil is the father of lies, for there is no truth within him. He is a thief, he comes to steal, kill, and destroy, but Jesus said he comes that we have life and that we have it more abundantly. Jesus can do exceedingly, abundantly, and above all that we could ask, according to the power that is working by him. Know who you are in Christ and the power and authority He has given us.

> *Scripture References*
> *2 Timothy 3:13*
> *2 Timothy 2:3-5*
> *Romans 8:31*
> *John 8:44*
> *John 10:10*
> *Psalms 34:19*

From the days of John the Baptist the kingdom of God sufferth violence and the violent take it by force. The power of God is greater than the forces of the enemy. God said in Psalms 34:19 that many are the affliction of the righteous, but the Lord delivers us out of them all. He did not say that to some, but He told them all.

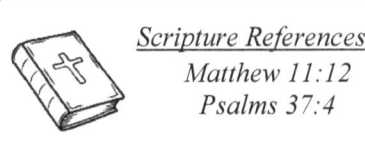

Scripture References
Matthew 11:12
Psalms 37:4

According to Hebrews 13:8, Jesus Christ, the same yesterday, today, and forever. God is going to get the glory. We must take the word and mix it with faith. God has promised that He has built His church upon the rock, and the gates of hell shall not prevail against it. The name of the Lord is a strong tower; the righteous ran into it, and they are safe.

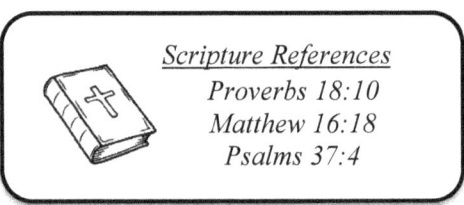

Scripture References
Proverbs 18:10
Matthew 16:18
Psalms 37:4

This is the confidence we have; if you ask anything according to his word, He heareth us, and if we know that He heareth us, then we know that we have the petitions that we desire of Him according to 1 John 5:14. God has made some promises unto us, and we fight the good fight. A fight to defeat the enemy. The enemy will not make it easy for us, but we have overcome this world, for greater is He in us than He in this world.

> *Scripture References*
> *1 John 4:4*
> *Romans 8:31*
> *Revelation 12:4*
> *Daniel 4:17*

There is more on our side than it is on their side. There are 2/3 of the angels with us. The Father, Son, and Holy Spirit are with us. If God be for us, who can be against us? God's for us is more than the world against us. We have the kingdom of God backing us. The kingdom of God does rule. It reminds me of Elijah and his servant, who said to his servant there be more with us than it is with them. So Elijah said to open his eyes, Lord. The Lord opened his servant's eyes, and he could see what Elijah was trying to tell him. May God open our eyes so that we can see. Especially what God is saying to us that we can have. If we believe and see it, we can have it.

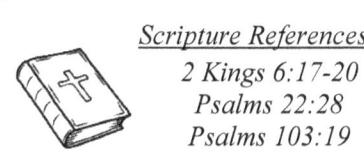

> *Scripture References*
> *2 Kings 6:17-20*
> *Psalms 22:28*
> *Psalms 103:19*

God will give, as I said earlier, specific directions and instructions for us to do and fulfill. It must be done precisely how God has instructed us to do it. Amen.

We will have to hear the voice of the Lord like never before. Satan is limited, but we know we have already won the battle and, indeed, the war. God is all-wise. He is all-wise, but He also has all the power in his hand. The Kingdom of God does rule. God is Lord Sabaoth. He helps us in the battle to give us victory. Expect miracles, miracles, miracles because that is what will happen in these last days.

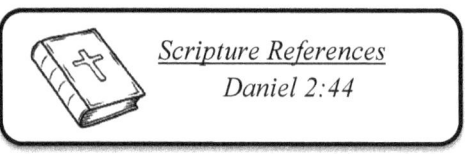

"With God, all things are possible when we believe."

Mark 9:23

Paul said all men have not faith. Jesus himself asked when He comes back, will He find faith in the earth? Let us not be like the five foolish virgins. Let us be like the five wise virgins who have enough oil when the bridegroom comes. But foolish virgins wanted some of the oil of the wise virgins. We must stay ready. King David said, teach us to number our days.

> *Scripture References*
> *Luke 18:1-8*
> *Matthew 25:1-13*
> *2 Thessalonians 3:1-2*
> *Psalms 90:12*
> *1 Thessalonians 5:19*

We are in some very fierce times. The warfare is tremendous, so we must pray without ceasing. Men are to always pray and not faint. As I said earlier in the book, the spirit of seduction and lust is very strong on the earth. The spirit of Jezebel is powerful. I have always said Jezebel is a witch. It's also a very rebellious spirit, for God said that rebellion is a spirit of witchcraft.

Witchcraft is powerful on earth. Satanic worship, mysticism, and psychic powers are heavy in the church. Witchcraft and many other spirits have been released, ever stronger on earth. God is getting ready to expose some things through His servants, the prophets, and the prophetess.

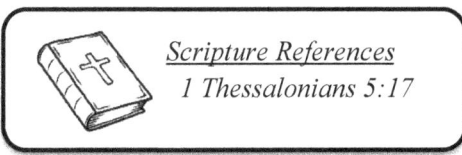

> *Scripture References*
> *1 Thessalonians 5:17*

According to Amos 3:7, God will do nothing on earth unless he first reveals it to his servants, the prophets. The prophets, apostles, and prophetesses are getting ready to escape obscurity. The glory of the Lord is willing to speak things we have never seen before. We are getting ready to see things we have never seen or heard of in our times. God said that some would be presented as angels of light, but they are angels of darkness. We will need to pray, seek God, and know Jesus like never before. There are many false prophets and false teachers, and they will increase. The spirit of the antichrist is powerful. I believe we are in the last days.

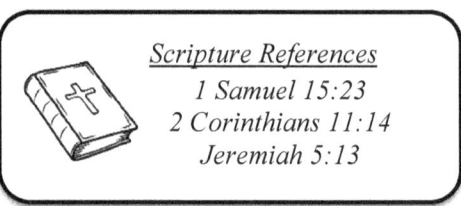

It's time to pray like never before. We must pray and get into the Word like never before. We must meditate upon the Word like never before; then, we shall make our way prosperous in our time. It's our season, and it's our time.

The victory is ours. We fight from victory to victory. The just shall live by faith. There is a pattern for the church of the living God. This book is about a call to prayer. It's time to pray like never before.

We must get on the wall and not come down. We must stay in an attitude of prayer. We must always pray and not faint. Jesus is coming back to a church without a wrinkle, a blemish, a spot, or not such things.

> *Scripture References*
> *Joshua 1:8*
> *Luke 18:1*
> *Ephesians 5:27*
> *2 Corinthians 2:14*
> *Nehemiah 4:6*

God bless and keep you and cause His face to shine upon you, beloved. Jesus loves you and always wants to give us victory. For it is always that God wants us to triumph in Christ Jesus. He has given us the authority and everything that we need. It is finished! The victory is ours. To God be the glory!

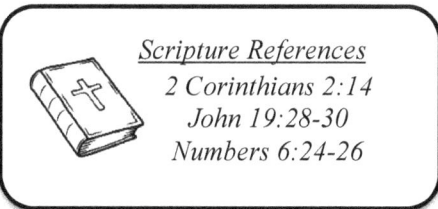

> *Scripture References*
> *2 Corinthians 2:14*
> *John 19:28-30*
> *Numbers 6:24-26*

The sons of Issachar knew God's timings and seasons and what Israel was to do. So, likewise, we need to seek God for our personal life and the church for the times and seasons.

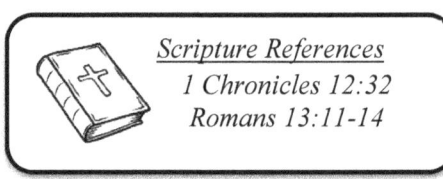

Scripture References
1 Chronicles 12:32
Romans 13:11-14

Know this, that harvest is plenteous, and laborers are few. Therefore, we must pray that the Lord of the harvest would send forth laborers in the harvest. Pray for laborers to go forth to your family and friends as well. Jesus said He would not return until his gospel had been preached in all nations, then shall the end come.

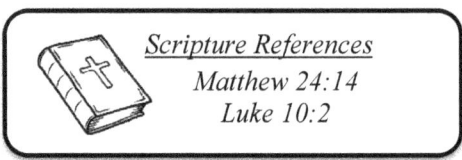

Scripture References
Matthew 24:14
Luke 10:2

Pray ye that you will be counted worthy to escape the things that would come upon this earth. This is because God said men's hearts would fail then for things that would come upon this earth.

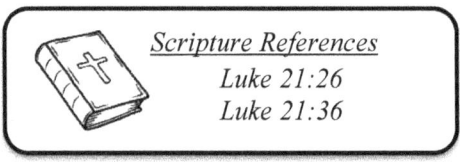

Scripture References
Luke 21:26
Luke 21:36

God has not given us a spirit of fear but of power, love, and a sound mind. Perfect love cast out all fear, for faith worketh by love. Ye have heard that it has been said, Thou shalt love thy neighbor and hate thy enemy. But I say unto you, love your enemies, bless them that curse you, do good to them that hate you, and pray for those that distally use and persecute you, that ye may be children of your Father which is in heaven, for He maketh his sun rise on the evil and the good and just and the unjust. We love those who love you. What rewards ye have and do not the heathens the same.

> *Scripture References*
> 1 John 4:18
> 2 Corinthians 13:5-13
> James 1:4
> 2 Timothy 1:7
> Matthew 5:43-48

According to Matthew 5:48, Be ye perfect even as your father in heaven is perfect. Sin shall not have dominion over us. In the epistles, the Apostle Paul told us to strive for perfection so that God would perfect those things that concern us. Being confident that He that hath begun a good work in you will complete until the day of Jesus Christ.

Paul, the apostle, said, I prayed and birthed you into God's Kingdom. He also said I travail until Christ is formed in you. We continually pray for people. It is not easy to see people come and not be transformed. We must pray until Christ is formed in them that they will become more like Jesus. That they and we can come to the full stature of Jesus Christ. The strong will bear the infirmity of the weak. We must pray for one another so that we can be healed.

> *Scripture References*
> Romans 6:14-21
> Philippians 1:6
> Philippians 3:12-21
> Psalms 138:8
> Romans 15:1
> James 5:16

"And for their sake, I sanctify myself. That they also may be sanctified through the truth. Thy Word is truth."

John 17:19

"The water of the Word washes us."

Ephesians 5:20

"Neither prays I for these alone me, but for those who shall believe me through their Word."

John 17:20

According to John 17:21-24, I and the Father that they all may be one as I and the Father are one. They also may be one in us, that the world may believe that thou hast sent me and the glory which thou gavest I have given them; not they may be one, even as we are one. I in them, and thou in me that they may be made perfect in one, and that the world may know that thou hast sent me; and thou hast loved them, thou hast loved me. Father, I will that them also, whom thou hast given me, be where I am that they behold my glory which hast given me for thou loveth me before the foundation of the world.

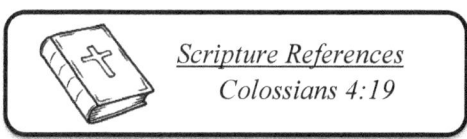

"Oh righteous Father, the world has not known thee, but I have known thee, and these have known that thee has sent me."

John 17:25

"And have declared unto them thy name and will declare it, and that wherewith thou hast loved me may be in them and I in them."

John 17:26

I remember, over 30 years ago, at the church, I was attending in my hometown, the Baptist church pastor asked me to do the thought for the morning. After much prayer, God gave me these scriptures: we need to pray for the body of Christ so that we would become one. In the prayer that Jesus prayed, we need to agree with His prayers. That prayer shall come to pass, not one only, but many members. All men will know that we are His disciples by loving one another. We have a love of God in us. It's shed abroad in our hearts by the Holy Ghost. We certainly don't want to be one whose love has waxed cold.

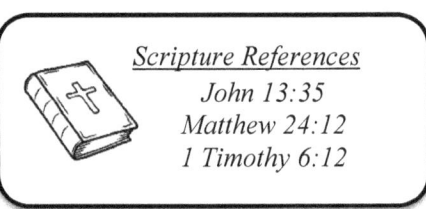

Scripture References
John 13:35
Matthew 24:12
1 Timothy 6:12

When Jesus returns, I must be ready. Should He tarry, or I go home to be with Him? I want to finish my course and hear Jesus say well done thou good and faithful servant; enter thou into what you have prepared for you.

We are in a time of warfare like never before. We learned how to fight the good fight of faith. We must fight on the offense rather than the defense. We must put on Christ, put on the whole armor of God.

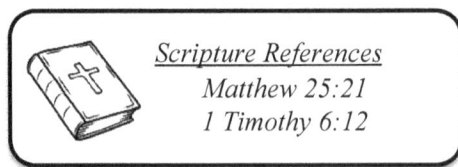

Scripture References
Matthew 25:21
1 Timothy 6:12

"Finally, my brethren, be strong in the Lord, and the power of his might. Put on the whole armor of God that ye may be able to stand against the devil's wiles."

Ephesians 6:10-11

For we wrestle not against flesh and blood, but powers and principalities, against the rulers of the darkness of this world, against spiritual wickedness in high places. Wherefore take unto you the whole armor of God that ye may be able to stand in the evil days, having done all to stand therefore for having your loins girt about with truth; having on the breastplate of righteousness and your feet shod with the preparation of the gospel of peace. Above all, take the shield of faith wherewith ye shall be able to quench all fiery darts of the wicked and take the helmet of salvation and the sword of the spirit, which is the Word of God. Praying always with all prayer and supplication in the Spirit and watching thereunto with all perseverance and supplication for all saints; and for me, that utterance may be given unto me, that I may open my mouth boldly, to make known the mystery of the gospel, for I am an ambassador in bonds that I may tell, but that ye may also know my ways and how I do.

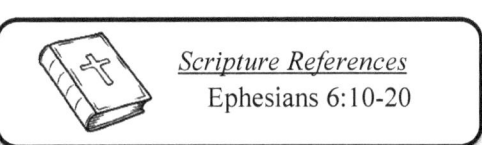

Scripture References
Ephesians 6:10-20

He means people when God says we are not fighting flesh and blood. But the enemy may use or speak through people to work through them. So God has given us power and authority.

Luke 10:19 says, Behold, God has given us power and authority. God has given us the ability to tread upon the scorpion serpent and, above all, the control of the enemy; it doesn't matter if it's demons or the power of darkness. We have power and authority over those forces of darkness. No weapon formed against us shall prosper, and every tongue that rises against us will not prosper, and every tongue that rises against us in judgment, he shall condemn and show it to be in the wrong.

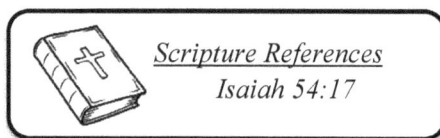
Scripture References
Isaiah 54:17

I was in a city here in America and met a precious lady, 108 years old, living in her own house, cooking her meals, and making her groceries. She told me, "If God is for you, no one can be against you," and shared some other things with me. A divine appointment, she said, I was supposed to meet you. She said she was supposed to come the next day but came that day instead. I am honored to meet such an extraordinary saint in the Lord. What a wonderful God we serve. She was walking without a cane.

How awesome and loving is our God? We must put our trust totally in the Lord. He will support us in perfect peace if we keep our minds on Him. We must fast and pray. I may never see her in this life again, but I will see her in heaven or eternity.

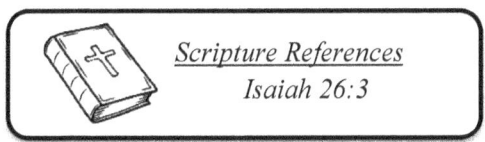

Scripture References
Isaiah 26:3

I sought for a man among them to make up the hedge and stand in the gap before thee that I should not destroy it, but I found none says Ezekiel 22:30. In countries and even this country, our families and even churches, we stand in the gap to make up a hedge over our family, self, community, and government. It is time for us to pray as we have never prayed before. It is time for all types of prayer; intercessory, supplication, and petition. Don't forget to worship and praise God.

King David was a great king. He was a man after the heart of God. When his wife Michal saw King David worshiping God, she got upset with him. God shut up her womb. King David let nothing or no one stop him from praising and worshiping God. King David knew God since he was a shepherd in the field. He pledged his life to Praise God. He killed a lion and bear and knew God had given Goliath into his hand. So Israel was afraid of the Philistines and giant Goliath. King David was not scared because he knew that God would deliver Goliath into his hand. He would not go into his strength but in the name of the Lord. If we are going to be victorious, we must believe in the power in his name, the blood, the Word, and who we are in Christ Jesus. King David said, is there not a cause?

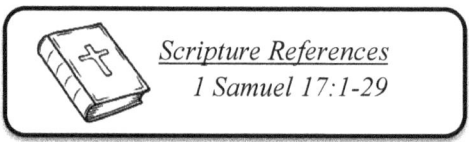

Scripture References
1 Samuel 17:1-29

If it was ever a time to pray, it's now. We must meditate on God's Word day and night; then, we shall make our way prosperous and successful. We must continually speak God's Word until the answer comes. Then continually speak God's word. We must constantly call those things that are not as though they were. God is sovereign. He is the creator of all things. He spoke this world into existence, and we can change things by saying God's Word when Jesus was led into the wilderness by the spirit to be tempted by the devil, forty days and forty nights as He fasted. Jesus was the word, but Jesus still spoke the Word every time the devil came to Him with a temptation. He defeated the devil every time by saying the Word of God. Satan is already defeated.

> *Scripture References*
> *Job 22:28*
> *James 5:17*
> *Matthew 4:1-11*
> *1 Kings 18:1-25*

We must enforce his defeat every time. The Word of God will defeat the devil. So it will be through the Word of God, the name of Jesus, and the blood of Jesus. Jesus was tempted at all points, just like we are. Elijah was a man of like passion, just like we are, but he defeated the prophets of Baal.

When Elijah told Ahab it would not rain for three and a half years, it didn't. When he prayed, God honored his prayers. Don't give up; don't stop praying. Keep praying. Keep seeking the Lord. Things may not always be easy. But keep the faith and keep seeking God.

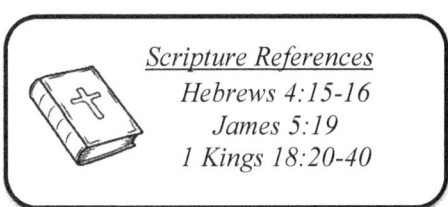

> *Scripture References*
> *Hebrews 4:15-16*
> *James 5:19*
> *1 Kings 18:20-40*

Sometimes, circumstances and spiritual forces can be stubborn, but you keep speaking. God's Word and casting down all imaginations and bringing every thought captive rendering it inoperable and bringing it into the obedience of Christ. Jesus will return when His enemies are made His footstool. So also, this gospel must be preached in all nations. Then shall the end come.

> *Scripture References*
> *2 Corinthians 10:5*
> *Hebrews 10:13*
> *Matthew 24:14*
> *Psalms 110:1*

Jesus prayed all night before He chose His disciples. Jesus would often go aside to pray in the mountains or the wilderness. We are in dangerous times now like never before. God said in His Word that evil would wax worse and worse. Therefore, we must strengthen ourselves in this hour and day like never before. Moses told Joshua in Joshua 1:7, only be thou strong and very courageous that thou mayest prosper according to all it the law, which Moses my servant commanded thee. Turn not from it to the right or the left that thou mayest prosper whatsoever thou may goest.

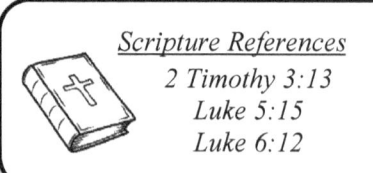

> *Scripture References*
> *2 Timothy 3:13*
> *Luke 5:15*
> *Luke 6:12*

I learned from walking with God that what you get by faith takes dedication to keep it because there is a thief. According to John 10:10 says, the thief comes to steal, kill and destroy, but I have come that you have life and that more abundantly. God wants us to have a good life, a blessed life. He doesn't want us to be in bondage. So I want to encourage some of you who are reading this book. Trust with all your heart and lean not to your understanding. You will live well again! God will restore all that the cankerworm, palmerworm, and locust have taken.

> *Scripture References*
> *Proverbs 3:5-8*
> *Joel 2:25-26*
> *Jeremiah 30:17*
> *Acts 30:3-13*

Scriptures

The Lord is my Shepherd I shall not want. He is Jehovah Jireh, my provider. He is Jehovah Rohi (my Shepherd). He is the God who looks ahead, provides for us, and meets my every need.

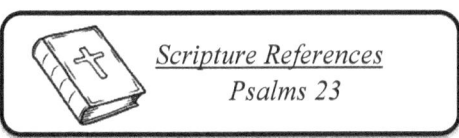
Scripture References
Psalms 23

My God shall supply all my needs according to his riches in Christ Jesus. Confess every day prayerfully; my harvest is on the way. I lack no good things. My harvest is on the way.

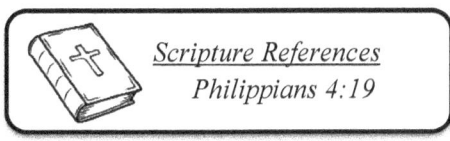
Scripture References
Philippians 4:19

God will do exceedingly, abundantly above all I ask or think. He is El Shaddai (all sufficient one).

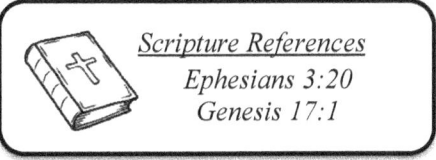
Scripture References
Ephesians 3:20
Genesis 17:1

With God, all things are possible to him that believes. Sometimes, you have to say and say it. I have never seen the righteous forsaken, nor his seed begging bread.

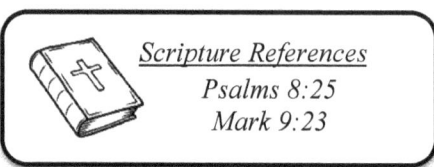

Scripture References
Psalms 8:25
Mark 9:23

He maketh me lie down in green pastures, leadeth me beside the still waters, and restored my soul. Jehovah Shalom, my prince of peace. In stillness and quietness, ye shall prosper.

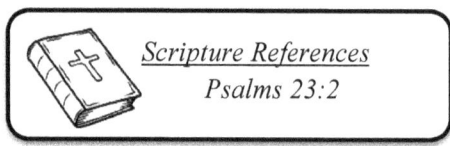

Scripture References
Psalms 23:2

By grace are ye saved through faith in Christ Jesus. God's grace is sufficient. He leadeth me in the path of righteousness for his namesake—Jehovah Tsidkenu (God of righteousness). The Lord, our shepherd, ye are righteous and complete in Christ.

Scripture References
Ephesians 2:8-9
2 Corinthians 12:9
Jeremiah 23:6
Jeremiah 33:16
Colossians 2:10
Ephesians 2:8

Though I walk through the valley of shadows of death for I will fear no evil for thou are with me, thy rod and thy staff, they comfort me; thy anointed my head with oil, my cup runneth over. Jehovah Shammah (He is always there).

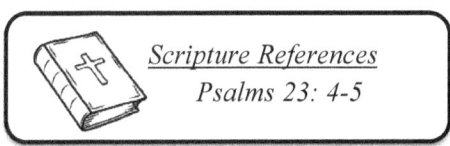
Scripture References
Psalms 23: 4-5

God can do exceedingly, abundantly above all that we could ask or think.

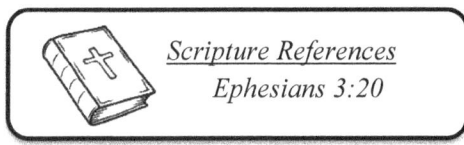
Scripture References
Ephesians 3:20

Thou preparest a table before me in the presence of my enemies. On that table is peace, joy, love, righteousness, prosperity, victory, grace, humility, forgiveness, truth, wisdom, passion for God, and the things of God.

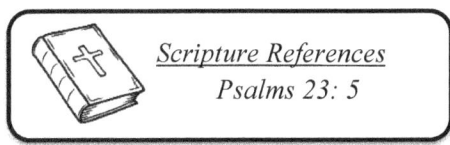
Scripture References
Psalms 23: 5

Salvation for children, family, and children to come. Faith to faith, strength to strength, glory to glory, prosperity to prosperity, victory to victory, joy to joy, love to love. Oh, to know the depth, height, and width of that love. Love covers a multitude of sins. I lay aside every weight and sin that so easily beset me—looking unto Jesus, the author and finisher of my faith—forgetting those things that are behind. The spirit of the Lord leads them that are the sons of God. I humble myself under the mighty hand of God that He may exalt me in due season. On that table is the favor of the Lord.

Scripture References
1 Peter 4:7
Hebrews 12:1-2
Philippians 3:13-14
Ephesians 12:18
Hebrews 8:18
1 Peter 5:6

So shall thy find favor and good understanding in the sight of God and man.

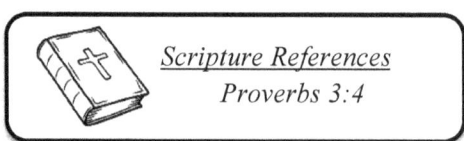

Scripture References
Proverbs 3:4

On that table is divine protection, long life I would live and finish strong. My latter days would be better than my former ones; on that table are health, wholeness, the good, and the blessed life. On that table, I endure hardness as a good soldier. On that table is revelation knowledge. On that table is peace.

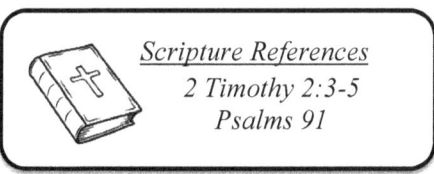
Scripture References
2 Timothy 2:3-5
Psalms 91

And it shall come to pass in that day, that his burden shall be taken away from off thy shoulder, and his yoke from off thy neck, and the yoke shall be destroyed because of the anointing.

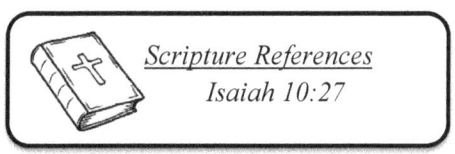
Scripture References
Isaiah 10:27

Jesus makes intercession for me daily. The feelings of my infirmities touch Him, and His compassion is new every morning. He turns my mourning into dancing, my ashes into beauty. The blood of Jesus cleanses me daily.

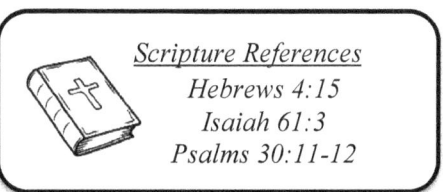
Scripture References
Hebrews 4:15
Isaiah 61:3
Psalms 30:11-12

The Lord is my portion, for in quietness and confidence is my strength. His mercies and compassion are new every morning.

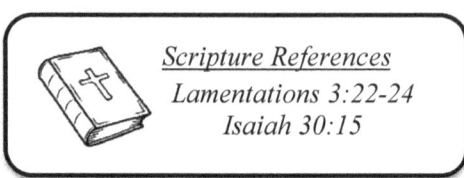

Scripture References
Lamentations 3:22-24
Isaiah 30:15

I have confidence in my savior. This is the confidence that I have in Him that if I ask anything according to His will, He hears me; if He heareth me, then I have the petitions that I ask of Him. I know that Jesus loves me and cares for me.

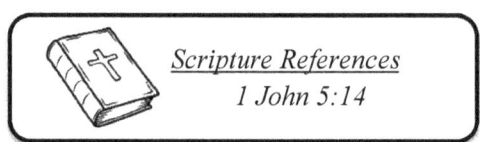

Scripture References
1 John 5:14

Many people have been in transition for years but have never transitioned to where God wants them to go. Whether in their ministry, business, job, family, or personal life. But many of you will transition into God's place for you. Some of you will be going to your next phase of ministry. No more will the church be in travail and unable to birth forth. When Zion travailed, she brought forth, and Paul said: I prayed and birthed you into the kingdom, and now I travailed that Christ may be formed in you. We will see more of the supernatural power of God than ever before.

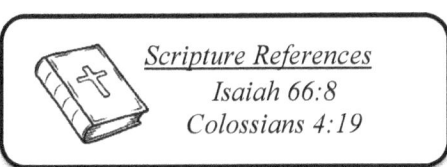

God works behind the scenes, making the crooked places straight and the rough places smooth. Many blessings that have been held up will come to many. Family members are going to be saved. Many are looking in the direction of change. They will experience the difference that they are looking for. Many of you will be stirred even in the midnight hours to seek God like never before. Some will even experience God in His glory. Some God will instruct, and some will get directions from the Holy Spirit. Follow them to the letter; don't go to the right or the left. God bless you. I trust that God will give you fresh revelations as you read this book, and you will never be the same. Peace and grace be with you.

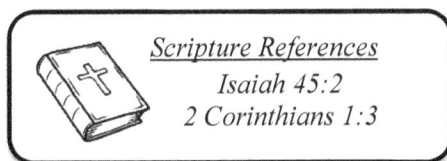

We must seek God like never before in this hour. We must seek God and search for Him with all of our hearts and receive the reward and study to show ourselves approved. A workman who needs not be ashamed but rightfully divides the word of truth. We, as ministers, must preach the gospel with authority and power and call the people to repent. King David made some mistakes, but he was quick to repent. King David loved God. He was the only person in the Bible that God said was a man after his own heart. King David was a mighty warrior. Not only in nature, but he was also a great spiritual warrior. King David was not only a great man of prayer but also a great worshiper and a great man of praise. Reading the Psalms and meditating on them inspire, encourage, enlighten you, and bring peace to your soul. Many of King David's Psalms are prayers to God. God stills the enemy; He binds kings and nobles on your behalf. King David was a prophet, a priest, and a king.

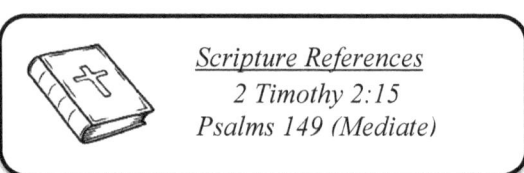

Scripture References
2 Timothy 2:15
Psalms 149 (Mediate)

When they attacked and burned Ziklag, King David asked the Lord what he should do. He encouraged himself in the Lord. He said to Abiathar, the Priest, bring me the ephod, and King David inquired of the Lord, and God said, go and recover all. After they gathered the spoil, they drove the cattle ahead and said, this is David's spoil. The enemy has taken much from many of us, and God wants us to seek Him and recover all the enemy has taken. Praise the Lord.

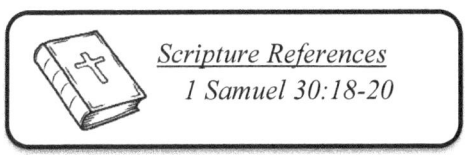

Scripture References
1 Samuel 30:18-20

Be glad then, ye children of Zion, and rejoice in the Lord your God, for He hath given you the former rain moderately, and He will cause to come down for you the rain, the former and the latter rain in the first month.

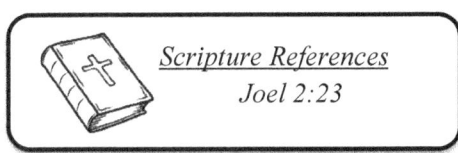

Scripture References
Joel 2:23

And I will restore to you the years that the locust hath eaten the cankerworm, the caterpillars, and palmerworm—my great army, which I sent among you. And ye shall eat in plenty and be satisfied and praise the name of your God that the name of the Lord, your God that hath dealt wondrously with you, and my people shall never be made ashamed. Ye shall know that I am amid Israel and that I am the Lord God, and none else and my people shall never be made ashamed, and I will pour my spirit upon all flesh, and your sons and your daughters shall prophesy. Your young men shall see visions, and your old men will also dream dreams upon the servants and the handmaidens in those days. Will I pour out my spirit, and will show wonders in the heavens above and fire in the Earth beneath, blood and fire and vapor of smoke.

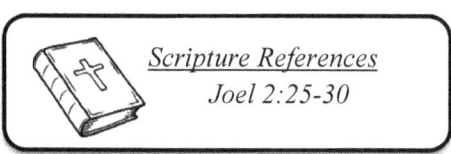

Scripture References
Joel 2:25-30

We need to seek the wisdom of God in our lives like never before. God will help us in this hour. We are indeed in the last of the last days. We must seek God while He is to be found. Seek Him every day and pray without ceasing.

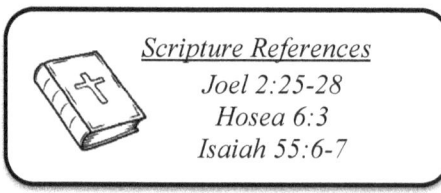

Scripture References
Joel 2:25-28
Hosea 6:3
Isaiah 55:6-7

Always stay in an attitude of prayer. May intercessory prayers and all types of prayers bring the presence of the Holy Spirit and answers to prayers.

God has given us some things to pray for; pray that we are counted worthy to escape these things that would come upon this earth, as many things are already happening, and yet more is to come. Pray ye that the Lord of the harvest would send forth laborers. Pray for all those in authority. Please pray for this church and the harvest like never before. Some countries desire a one-world government. The spirit of the antichrist and the one-world government is stronger now than ever. Racism is at an all-time high, and none of these things should not be found among God's people. We are the righteous of God in Christ Jesus. I trust and pray that Americans will repent and turn back to God. We need Jesus to intervene in the affairs of men like never before.

Scripture References
Luke 21:36
Matthew 9:38
2 Timothy 2:1-3
1 Thessalonians 5:19

We are in some profound and troublesome times. We are in the times God talks about in Matthew: 24:14 chapter, but the end is not yet. This gospel must be preached in all nations; then shall the end come. God said, pray ye the Lord of the harvest would send forth laborers, for the laborers are few, but the harvest is plentiful. We need to pray for severe protection and provision prayers for our missionaries. I am a missionary myself with a global vision. My heart is not only for America but for the nations. God said the Kingdom of God suffers violence, and the violent take it by force. Pray that God sends laborers worldwide to seek the Lord in the prayer of intercession for the nations. Pray that God would raise laborers for the harvest, especially with COVID-19. Pray that we get the answer. We need fervent prayers. Many times people will pray when they get into a desperate situation. Men are always to pray and not faint. We must pray like never before and study the word like never before.

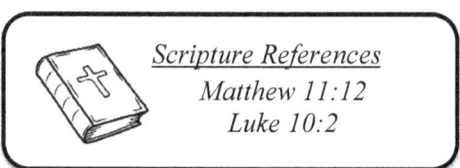

Scripture References
Matthew 11:12
Luke 10:2

Study to show thyself approved, a workman that need not be ashamed, rightly dividing the word of truth. We must study the word and have an understanding and revelation knowledge of who we are. We must meditate on the word, observe, and do what is right. We must do it day and night; then, we shall prosper. We must confess and speak the word in prayer daily.

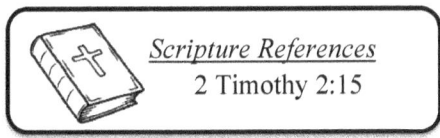

"Thou shall decree a thing, and it is established unto thee. God said, command ye me."
Job 22:28

We can demand the word, but when we speak it in faith and believe it, we can have what we say.

If we speak to mountains in our life, it has to obey. Sometimes, we have to say it, but if we dare to believe it in our hearts, then situations or circumstances must abide by the word. When Jesus was fasting for 40 days and 40 nights in the wilderness, He said that it is written. We can defeat the enemy through confessing and standing on the word.

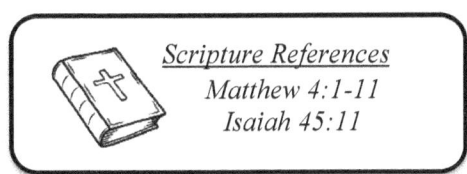

Example: Philippians 4:19: If God says He will meet all of our needs according to his riches in glory by Christ Jesus, He will meet all our needs if we believe in Him. We will see many miracles, supernatural provisions, and healings.

The enemy fights God's people the most in finances and health. But He promised to help us, and He will, but we must trust Him in everything.

> *"God is not a man that He should lie."*
> *Numbers 23:19*

"I am the way and the truth. No man comes to the Father except but by me."
John 14:6

This couldn't be said enough. We must confess God's Word and pray for revelation and understanding. Get wisdom, and with all thy knowledge, gain understanding. To get answers from God, we must pray the prayer of faith.

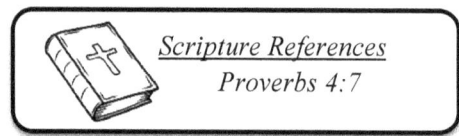

Faith cometh by hearing and hearing by the Word of God. I know God answers prayers, and we must learn to make the right choices. God has given us dominion over the earth and has also given us authority over our situations, circumstances, and things; He has also given us authority over demon spirits.

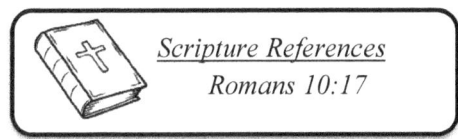
Scripture References
Romans 10:17

Luke 10:19: Behold, I have given you the power to tread upon serpents and scorpions and over the enemy's strength.

We walk by faith and not by sight. We must contend for the faith that was once delivered among the saints. Jude, the servant of his Jesus Christ and brother of James, to them sanctified by God the Father and preserved in Christ Jesus and called, mercy to you, and peace and love be multiplied.

Beloved, when I gave all diligence to write unto you of the common salvation, it was needful for me to write unto you that you should earnestly contend for the faith that was once delivered unto the saints. Their certain men crept in unawares, who were before old ordained to this condemnation. Ungodly men, turning the grace of our God into lasciviousness and denying the only Lord and our Lord Jesus Christ. I will therefore put you in remembrance though ye will know how the Lord, having saved the people out of Egypt, afterward destroyed them that believe not and the angels who kept not their first estate but left their open habitations; He hath reserved in everlasting chains under darkness unto the judgment of the great day.

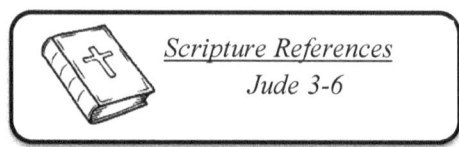

Scripture References
Jude 3-6

God will judge the saved and the unsaved. We must judge ourselves so that we will not be judged. The Word of God is our mirror. Jesus said when He comes, will he find faith in the earth. To every man or woman or child born again, God has given a measure of faith. The things happening on the earth are the beginning of the things that are coming upon the earth, the great tribulation. We must pray that we are counted worthy to escape these things. We must not be like the five foolish virgins. We must get the word in our hearts with fundamental knowledge. It must not depart from our eyes; we must meditate on the word day and night. We must pray without ceasing.

> *Scripture References*
> *1 Thessalonians 5:17*
> *Jude 1:3-6*
> *2 Corinthians 5:7*
> *Romans 12:3*
> *Luke 18:8*
> *Luke 21:36*
> *1 Corinthians 11:31*
> *Job 22:28*

As the church, we must come to another level, a higher level in Christ. We must seek the Lord. We will see some of the greatest miracles we have ever seen. The Lord will indeed exceed that of the former house. The apostles and prophets will also come to the scene and the forefront. The church is built on the apostles, prophets, and Jesus Christ, our chief and head cornerstone. He is the stone that the builder rejected, and still, today, many are rejecting.

> *Scripture References*
> *Act 4:11*
> *Haggai 2:9*
> *Psalms 118:22*
> *Matthew 21:42*
> *Ephesians 2:20*
> *Matthew 21:33-43*

"I am the way, the truth, and the life: No man can come to the Father except by me."
John 14:6

Years ago, in a meeting with a sister called Debra, I told her about the women and men there; I saw people praying like never before and so many people. We are in the last days. But there will be a falling away. All of creation is waiting on the manifestation of the sons of God. The glory of the latter shall be greater than that of the former. We will fight great battles but see and experience great victories, for we are overcome by the blood of the lamb and the word of our testimonies. We fight from victory to victory, faith to faith, and glory to glory. God's church will walk in boldness; for the righteous is as bold as a lion. Evil is all around, but God will protect us if we trust Him. Plead the blood, apply the blood, and sprinkle. In the name of Jesus, there is power in His Word, His name, and the blood of Jesus and praise. And beloved, none of these things will ever lose its power.

Put and keep your armor on; put on Christ. If I didn't know who I am in Christ, have His word in me, and have Him already in me, I would not have made it this far. While traveling, I met a precious lady in Missouri who was 108 years old. She was very sharp, making her grocery. Her daughter told me she lived in her own house as well. What an honor that God would allow me to meet one of His precious saints to be on the earth for so long and live for Him. I remember the word she said: if God is for you, who can be against you? This was about six years ago, and she also gave me another Word from the Lord. I received the word that she gave me.

> *Scripture References*
> *Haggai 2:9*
> *Romans 8:19*
> *Psalms 124:1*
> *Romans 8:31*
> *Revelation 12:11*
> *Proverbs 28:1*
> *Romans 7:1-17*
> *2 Corinthians 3:18*

We must seek the righteousness of God first, and everything else will be added unto us. Then, we must speak God's Word until our needs are manifested in our lives. Sometimes, we have to say it until it manifests or gets into our hearts.

> *Scripture References*
> *Matthew 6:33*

I have learned from walking with God that it would take faith to keep if you got it by faith. Because Satan is a thief, he comes to steal, kill, and destroy, but Jesus, I go so that you have life and that more abundantly. Jesus defeated the devil in the wilderness with the Word of God, and we're going to beat him. It is the Word. Glory to God. The promise of God is yea and Amen.

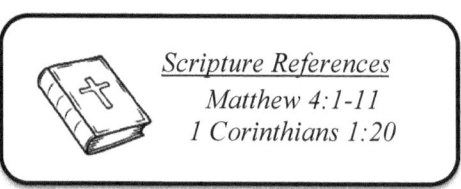

Scripture References
Matthew 4:1-11
1 Corinthians 1:20

We should not only read this chapter but also meditate on it until it becomes real in our hearts. We must continuously pray in the spirit and with understanding. Pray for God's will.

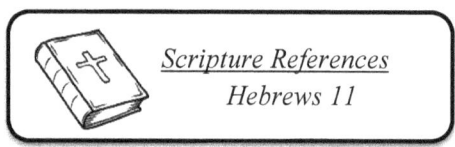

Scripture References
Hebrews 11

A good man leaves an inheritance for his children's children. The wealth of sinners is laid up for the just or the righteous. The blessing of the Lord maketh rich and addeth no sorrow.

Scripture References
Proverbs 10:22
Proverbs 13:22

Christ hath delivered us from the law's curse. For the blessing of Abraham is ours. God made Abraham rich. God blessed Abraham and made him very rich. Amid famine, we would be prosperous. Isaac sowed in that land during a famine, and God made Isaac very rich, as did his father, Abraham. Isaac sowed in the land and received 100-fold. Trust God to give you double for all your labor, as He did Job.

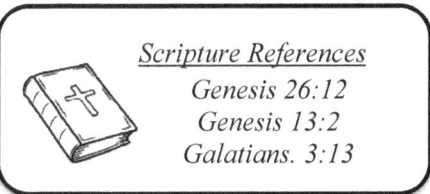

Scripture References
Genesis 26:12
Genesis 13:2
Galatians. 3:13

Trust God to give us houses; we didn't build houses filled with good things and vineyards we didn't plant. Read and meditate on the Deuteronomy 28th.

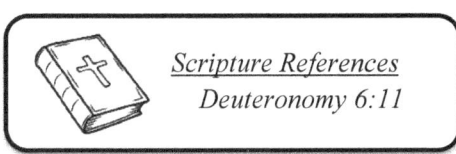

Scripture References
Deuteronomy 6:11

In Genesis, the Philistines kept closing up the wells, but Isaac didn't quit until he dug a well, and they did not stop up his well anymore. The name of the well was called Rehoboth. Remember and mediate how when the Philistines attacked the city. David inquired of the Lord, and God told him to go and recover all. The prophet Isaiah said none say restore. But the prophet Joel said God would restore all that the cankerworm and the palmerworm the locust hath taken. God promised that His people would never be made ashamed. Press for the prize of the higher calling in Christ Jesus.

Scripture References
Genesis 26:22
Genesis 18:26
Joel 2:25-26
1 Samuel 30:1
Isaiah 42:22

We are co-laborers with Christ. We are joint heirs with Christ. Pray for revelation. Turn away from your sins and turn to Jesus with all your heart, soul, and mind. Get God's Word in your heart.

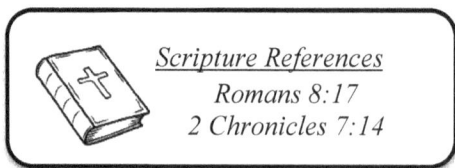

Scripture References
Romans 8:17
2 Chronicles 7:14

"Faith comes by hearing and hearing by the Word of God."
Romans 10:17

"Study to show yourself approved, a workman that need not be ashamed rightfully during the word of truth."
2 Timothy 2:15

"My people perish for lack of knowledge because you have forgotten me. I will also forget you and your children."
Hosea 4:6

What we are doing, we seek God and His Word. We are doing it not only to be blessed and increase our faith but also for our children and future generations. Seeking God and studying the word should be a lifestyle for the rest of our lives. As we seek the Lord, he will make himself more real to us, and we will know what to do in every given situation and circumstance. King David was a mighty king who made mistakes, but he was a good person and quickly repented once he knew he had sinned. We will see more miracles as we continue to study God's Word and seek His favor. So we must prepare ourselves for what's coming upon this earth in this last hour; so that our faith would be strong and in the power of his might.

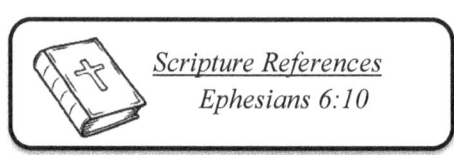

Scripture References
Ephesians 6:10

"Seek ye first the kingdom of God and His righteousness, and everything else will be added unto us."
Matthew 6:33

We are righteous in Christ Jesus. If we are Christians, the blood of Jesus cleanses us from all unrighteousness. If we hide sin in our hearts, God will not hear us. One person in the Bible that God said was a man after his heart. David was a prophet, priest, and king. David's men wanted to stone him when they saw that the city was burned. David had taught the very men to be mighty warriors and blessed them. However, King David sought the Lord and encouraged himself in the Lord. King David told them to bring him his ephod; only a priest was allowed to wear it. The Lord told him to go and recover everything. I believe the church will get into a place with God where we seek the Lord, hear his voice plainly, and obey him. I believe the church pastor and ministers will encourage their people to seek the Lord like never before. There is a pattern to church. There was a pattern to building Noah's Ark, the temple, and the early church, and God had a design for the church in the last days. God has called His church to be a glorious church. A church of signs and wonders and miracles. The church needs to move in the gift of the spirits. We need the anointing of the apostles and prophets in the church. Jesus did a lot of praying. Sometimes, He prayed all night long. Many times, He prayed alone. Particularly before His next assignment.

Scripture References
Luke 6:12
John 5:19-20
John 4:4
John 12:49
1 Samuel 30:1
1 Samuel 30:7-26
Romans 5:1
Ephesians 6:10

Jesus said, I only do what I see my father do. Jesus knew He had to go through Samaria and that He would meet the women at the well. If we sought the Lord, He would direct us to the spirit of God daily in what we do. When Paul and Silas were in prison, they sang praises to God, and the angels of the Lord delivered them out of jail.

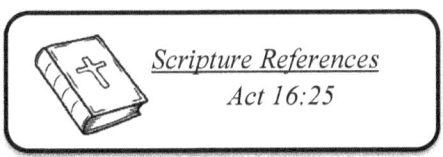

Scripture References
Act 16:25

When they had killed James, the brother of Jesus, they were going to kill Peter. But the church sought the Lord, and God delivered Peter. Peter was asleep, but his Angel woke him up. When Peter opened the door, Roda said an angel at the door. But they thought it was his Angel. God will do some miraculous things again like we have not seen in our days. There are going to be creative miracles. Jesus said He would not return until the restitution of all things. He is coming back for a glorious church, a church without spots, wrinkles, or blemishes. God is holy, and everything about God is sacred.

> *Scripture References*
> *Ephesians 2:6*
> *1 Peter 1:16*
> *Acts 12:5-12*
> *Acts 3:21*
> *Ephesians 5:25*

Follow peace and holiness with all men without which no man shall see my face. Many people have lost family and some friends, jobs, homes, and apartments during this pandemic. During this time, I stood to lose everything that I had. But some people in the church had said negative things. I stood on God's Word. I still believe God would supernaturally provide for my family and me and divinely protect us. Please meditate and read Psalms 91 daily for the rest of your life. Get it in your heart and confess it with your mouth. Answers or provisions will not just appear; we must pray for them. Pray for leaders in our communities, churches, America, and worldwide. God will hear the cry of his people. Trust me; God will hear and answer your prayers.

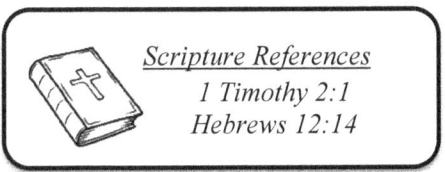

Scripture References
1 Timothy 2:1
Hebrews 12:14

The Word of God must not return void but will accomplish what it said it would do. His promises are yes and amen. I trust God that this book will bless you as much as it has blessed me writing it. God bless you, and may God do great things in your life.

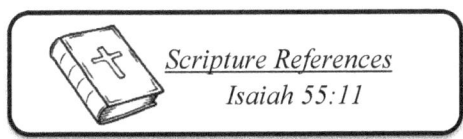

Scripture References
Isaiah 55:11

Seek the scriptures. In them, I think you will find eternal life. You will find God when you search for Him in your heart. Some of you will receive miracles like never before seen in your life as you seek the Lord. He is going to show Himself strong.

Pray that the eyes of the believers will open and ears to hear what God is saying in this hour. Also, pray for the Lord to raise the prophets and apostles. The church is built on the apostles and prophets and Jesus Christ, the chief apostle.

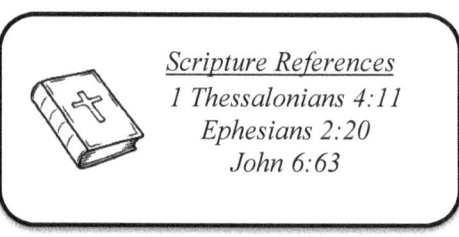

Scripture References
1 Thessalonians 4:11
Ephesians 2:20
John 6:63

Jesus is still making intercession for the church, so let's join Him and pray more frequently. Stand on Paul's Word in prayer. Call those things that are not as though they were. Call yourself blessed, righteous, and accessible.

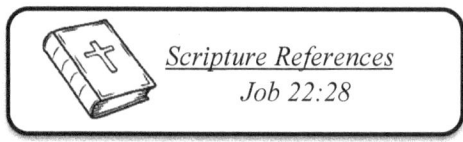

Scripture References
Job 22:28

Find scriptures to meet your or your family's or friend's needs, and do warfare. Isaiah42:13 says God is a man of war. II Chronicles 20:15 tells that the battle is the Lord's. Seek God, and find out what God wants you to do.

When one of the disciples asked Jesus how many times we must forgive, Jesus said 70 times 7. Go. Therefore, brother or sister, enemy or someone sins as or of it. We are to forgive them 70 times 7 in a day, then. Jesus said if we forgive not men for their trespasses, neither will He forgive you.

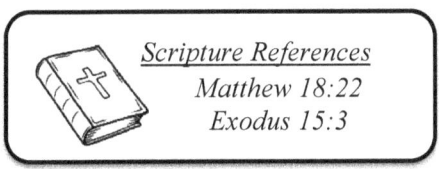

Scripture References
Matthew 18:22
Exodus 15:3

And answering said unto them. Have faith in God. For verily I say unto you, That whosoever shall say unto this mountain, Be thou removed and be thou cast into the sea and shall not doubt in his heart, but shall believe that those things which he saith shall come to pass, he shall have whatsoever he saith. Therefore, I say unto you, what things soever ye desire when you pray, believe that you receive them, and ye shall have them. And when ye stand praying, forgive if ye sin against any. Your father, also in heaven, may forgive your trespasses. We should not just be a constant doormat for people to walk over us and cause us to hurt. We must forgive them, no matter what. King David said if I hide iniquity in my heart, God will not hear me. So let's ensure our prayers are not hindered because of unforgiveness in our hearts. God tells us in His Word that faith worketh by love. He also tells us to love the Lord with all our hearts and mind and love our neighbors as yourself. On these hang the law. No, we do not live by the law but by grace. By grace are we saved, not of ourselves lest anyone as shall boast. The Lord is doing a quick work.

> *Scripture References*
> Matthew 22:40
> Mark 12:30-31
> Matthew 6:15
> Galatians 5:6
> Matthew 22:37
> Psalms 66:18
> Ephesians 2:8
> 1 Chronicles 28:23
> Mark 11:22-26

I have fought many battles, mainly since I have been in Tulsa, Oklahoma, and have seen many victories in every area of my life. My job transferred from my home state to Tulsa. My mother was a prophetess. I remember she said to me that it was God's will for me to come to Tulsa, but the following year, that is what God hath said to me. They kept pressing me to come that year, but I agreed with my mother. I also remember my mother saying it was a dark cloud over Tulsa. I also heard another prophet say those exact words. When I got on that job, I was harassed a lot. I remember when I saw my co-workers. I told one of the sisters in Christ that we were going to one of the Bible schools here. I said, you see that lady, she is a witch. I knew the lady was a witch. I also knew that she would come against me. But I was not afraid. I knew that neither she nor the others could win because greater is he that is in me than he that is in the world. No weapon formed against me shall prosper, and everything that rises against me in judgment, God shall condemn and be proven to be in the wrong. I looked at her and said in my heart, a fight you want, you will get, but you won't win.

I had all this occurring on the job, creating severe injuries. They would always put me in areas with a lot of standing and heavy lifting. One day in a safety meeting, one of the supervisors said that the businesspeople said they would not have their employees pick up those heavy sacks; some were up to 100 lbs. We were required to be able to lift 70 lbs. But they overfilled them and wouldn't pull them after I got off the machine. I still had to work in that area. A teacher worked there; she knew it was wrong, and she didn't appreciate it. She said the next time you do that; I will go for you. Sure enough, she did when he came over to send me to that area; all she said was, I'll go. The harassment was outrageous. The pain from the accident was excruciating. I saw a lot of specialists. Every specialist said I was not going to live. I reached the point where I could not even walk.

Several vertebrates were damaged, and I had bilateral carpal tunnel and developed a cyst on my right hand from all the heavy lifting and repetitive lifting and working. I had different ministers pray for me. I didn't get my healing right then, but I kept the faith. I kept praying, seeking the Lord daily. I knew that not being able to get relief was an unusual situation, but I didn't give up. I kept the faith. I kept praying and kept believing in God that I would be healed. Every specialist told me that I was going to die. All of the specialists said they had done all they could do. So I said, "Why should I keep coming to you?'" He said I needed to see a doctor. I was not able to walk. I have always been a healthy person. I knew unless I received a miracle, I wasn't going to live. The doctors kept telling my employer that I could not work and was totally disabled, but they kept putting pressure on the doctor to release me for work.

I knew I was in a spiritual war, but I was determined to win. I remember in my apartment; I could see demonic activity. I remember it was so fierce. I asked the Lord to help me. Another time, I prayed for war angels that were real. I knew when God sent me help. Angels are real. Sometimes, we need their help or assistance. God has sent us angels to help fight in battles. In the end, God supernaturally healed me from all incurable symptoms! It was a miracle.

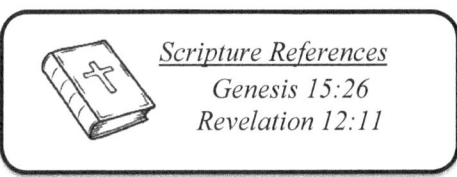
Scripture References
Genesis 15:26
Revelation 12:11

God is a man of war. He does not lose a war or battle. He always wins. We must fight to win.

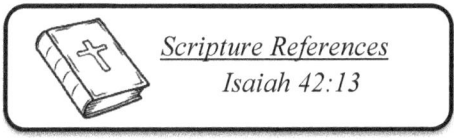
Scripture References
Isaiah 42:13

"Nay, in all things, we are more than conquerors."
Romans 8:37

It is always God that causes me to triumph in Christ Jesus. This is because God loves us so much and is for us, not against us. He wants us to succeed, win, and bring honor and glory to Him by obedience to His Word.

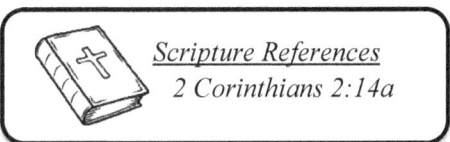
Scripture References
2 Corinthians 2:14a

"Declare a decree, and it shall be established unto you."
Job 22:28

Sometimes, I have to speak it over and over again. To take a stand and having done all to stand whatever comes against us. Seek the kingdom of God and His righteousness, and everything else shall be added unto you. We are righteous in Christ Jesus. We must know who we are in the power and authority that God has given us. If God says we continue in faith, we can do it. We are new creatures in Christ Jesus. Elijah was a man of passion, just like we are.

> *Scripture References*
> *Matthew 6:33*
> *James 5:17*
> *2 Corinthians 5:17*
> *Ephesians 6:13*

The Word of the Lord shall not depart out your mouth thou shall meditate on it both day and night then should make thy prosperous and thou shall have success. You must seek God both day and night. Say and say until it manifests. It is beautiful to have fellowship with God as you communicate with God and God talks to you. I thank God for that relationship. I have traveled a lot, both nationally and internationally, but never went out without prayers. I have seen the hand of God in many situations. This lady had a hospital band on her arm when I was in Cincinnati, OH. So I asked her if she was alright. She said no, my nerves were so bad. I have a son that causes so much trouble. She was concerned that he would get killed or into a lot of trouble, so I began ministering to her. By the time I finished, I had shared the gospel with her husband and daughter as they came out of the store. So I ministered to them, and they accepted the Lord. The teenage daughter said this is what we needed. Hallelujah!! Glory to God! He that winneth souls are wise. The angels rejoice over the person that comes to the Lord. I have traveled to many states but have seen God do beautiful things. I believe it comes out of prayer life and relationships with God.

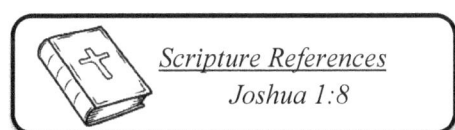

Scripture References
Joshua 1:8

Six years ago, I was in Clearwater, Florida and I met this lady and sometimes saw her on the bus. She told me she was homeless—a precious lady from the Islands. So I said you need to have a place to stay. I saw such an urgency that she needed a place to stay, and compassion rose within me. So when I saw her again, God provided her with a place to stay.

She knew it was a miracle. When I spoke to that lady, I knew God would get the glory, and He did. God is going to make some divine appointments in some of your lives. Expect miracles; expect God to do something good in your lives; expect the favor of God. When you speak God's Word in faith, mountains got to move; lack has got to move; sickness got to move. Anything that does not line up with God's will has to move.

> *"With God, all things are possible when we believe."*
> Mark 9:23

God is faithful, so we must believe in God. Your faith will be tried, but we must dare to believe God for the impossible. The enemy wanted to sniff me out when every doctor said I wouldn't live. But for over 30 years, none of the sicknesses or illnesses have returned. I stand on the scripture Nahum 1:9. I will continue to stand for the rest of my life. While I was also in Clearwater, Florida, during the same trip, I was out working and met this lady who had pancreatic cancer. So I prayed with her and found out that she also had bladder cancer.

But I saw her brother, who was a lawyer. He said you prayed for my sister; she had a death warrant. We know she found a miracle healing. Thank you, Jesus!

But when she got some tests run, they could not find pancreatic cancer. Glory to God! Hallelujah! I prayed with a lady from my home state who had an inoperable brain tumor. I met her husband sitting in a little riding cart because I couldn't walk. I looked at some bread, and he walked to the bread aisle. He asked me how I could tell if the bread was fresh. Could you share with me how to know if it's fresh? He said, my wife has an inoperable brain tumor. I want you to call and pray with her. While he was talking, he was writing her cell number. My brain was trying to think that I was in the spirit. But I had to understand what God had for me to do. So I said I will, but I couldn't say when, so I called her and prayed. God worked a miracle in that lady's life. The presence of God was so strong. God healed that lady. She said I got to get some tests run. Well, praise God, she went to get the tests run, and we talked again, and they could not find the tumor in her brain or lungs. I didn't know it was in her lungs, either. But God is still the God of miracles. But we have not seen anything yet. Pray for this country. Pray for and intercede that God would raise the prophets and apostles. There is a pattern to the church. We are in a spiritual war like never before.

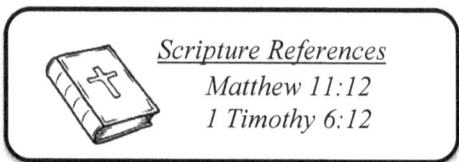

We must fight the good fight of faith. The just shall live by faith. We are not fighting flesh and blood but power and principalities. The kingdom of God is suffering violence, but the violent take it by force. We are in warfare like never before. Just know this. We win! It is always God that causes us to triumph in Christ Jesus. Nay, we are more than conquerors through Him that loves us in all things. Continually call those things that are not as we thought they were. The light of God indeed shines upon our path. We must pray that God would send forth laborers of the harvest. We must pray for the former and the latter rain. We must search the scriptures to find eternal life in them. So a man thinks in his heart, so is he. Jehoshaphat sought the Lord, and the Lord gave instructions through his prophet. God said to send Judah.

The praises went out saying the Lord is good and his mercy endureth forever. The battle was won, and they spent three days gathering the spoil! We should not only expect God to win the battle but receive the spoils. The battle is not yours but the Lord's! We must seek God more. The old saints used to say that blessings come down when praises go up. When we praise God for the answer before it comes, that's our faith, believing that we receive it before it happens. Faith without works is dead. Faith is the substance of things hoped for, the evidence of things not seen. God is still working miracles. Jesus Christ, the same yesterday, today, and forever. Don't give up. Stand. Having done all, stand. Keep the faith. God will come through. Believe that He would. When all the specialists said I would not live, I kept standing on God's word. Here I stand; God healed me of several incurable diseases. I have traveled to several nations of the world. I traveled to several countries in Europe, including Paris, Switzerland, Brussels, Belgium, and Mexico, twice. Also, several countries in communist China. To God be the Glory. Many people were delivered, healed, and saved in each nation I traveled to. When I taught at Bible college in Switzerland, a young lady broke down and wept, saying I see Jesus in your eyes. To God be the glory for the great things He has done, is doing, and will do. Pray for the former and latter rain in your life: your church, your family, this nation, and the world. Believe in God for a worldwide revival. Let it start with us. Lord, Holy Spirit, do a work in us that only You can do. God is looking for someone with whom He can show Himself strong. They that know their God shall be victorious and do great exploits. Make prayers and confessing God's Word a lifestyle, a way of life for the rest of your life. I hope that as you read, study, and confess God's Word, this book will bless you as much as it has me.

> *Scripture References*
> *2 Corinthians 2:14a*
> *Psalms 119:103*
> *Romans 8:37*
> *Luke 10:2*
> *Revelation 20:15*
> *Hosea 6:3*
> *Joel 2:23*
> *Jude 1:2*
> *2 Chronicles 7:3*
> *Psalms 136:1-3*
> *John 5:39*
> *Hebrews 11:1*
> *James 2:17-18*
> *Proverbs 23:7*
> *2 Chronicles 16:9*
> *Hebrews 13:8*
> *Daniel 11:32b*
> *2 Chronicles 20:21*

I have seen people delivered, humbled, healed, and blessed through prayer. For example, I was having problems with my knee and was in a lot of pain, so I was in a riding cart making groceries. This man walks up to me. I went over to the bread rack. So he walked over, picked up a loaf of bread, and said, do you know how to tell if a loaf of bread is fresh? I said no. Then he proceeded to say to me. But then he told me that his wife had an inoperable brain tumor and wanted me to call and pray for her.

God is awesome. So, I am trying to think I am in a riding cart because I can't walk around the store to make groceries. After all, the pain was so great. But I told him, I can't tell you when, but I will call your wife and pray for her. Come to find out; we were from the same state. I did give her a call, and we prayed; the power of God was so strong. I prayed that prayer in the name of Jesus and commanded that lady to be healed. She said, "I am healed. I am healed." Before we hung up, she said, "I was getting ready for a check-up." Sure enough, she said they could not find that tumor or anything in her lungs. I didn't know she had it in her lungs as well. To God be the glory for the great things He has done, is doing, and will do. There was another case in Florida. A lady with pancreatic cancer.

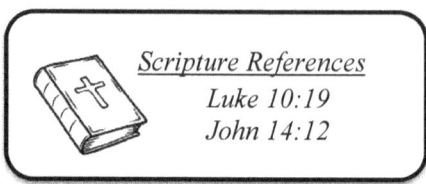

I prayed with her, and God healed her. Her brother, an attorney, told me that she had gotten healed. He told me; we knew she had a death sentence, which he was trying to say we knew she was dying. Attorneys are very analytical and intelligent. What a testimony to him and his family. I give God all glory and honor, all praise. I had never gone out traveling before. I spent much time in prayer and the word. Sometimes, it can be challenging work, but God has been good. Thank God for His favor. So shall we find acceptance and good understanding in the sight of God and man? Everything that I lay my hand to prosper in the name of Jesus. It is always God that causes us to triumph in Christ Jesus. Nay, in all things, we are more than conquerors.

> *Scripture References*
> *Deuteronomy 30:9*
> *Deuteronomy 29:9*
> *Proverbs 3:4*
> *Psalms 1:3*
> *2 Corinthians 2:14a*
> *Romans 8:37*

There are negative people in the church, so be careful who you talk to or ask to pray for you. If a person says a thing in agreement, then something negative happens when they turn their back. They are not in agreement. There are realms you go to in prayer. King David was aware of that. He said deep calls unto deep. King David knew God in such a way that many saints don't know today. David was a king, prophet, and priest. King David knew how to encourage himself in the Lord and get victory. A lady wanted to die because she had lost some of her children. So they had to put her in the hospital because she did not want to live. We prayed, and she got out of the hospital in a day or two. One of the ladies on the prayer line had problems with her eyes, and they swelled a lot.

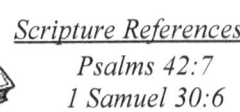

> *Scripture References*
> *Psalms 42:7*
> *1 Samuel 30:6*

We prayed, and the swelling went down almost entirely before she got off the prayer line. Praise God. Another lady we prayed for was her grandson, who got a concussion playing football and was very serious. God healed him, and he is doing fine. Another lady was very depressed and kept herself in the dark house and stayed in bed.

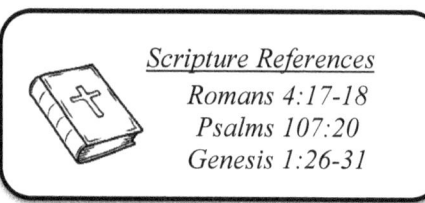

Scripture References
Romans 4:17-18
Psalms 107:20
Genesis 1:26-31

I was going through some memories and phone numbers, and I felt led to call her. Come to find out, she had a double mastectomy, both breasts removed. I asked if she wanted me to pray, and she said yes. We prayed, and she said she felt so much better. She would get up and put some clothes on and open her blinds. Praise God for deliverance. He sent His Word and healed them and delivered them from all destruction. God, Himself, called those things that are not as though they were. We need to know how to call these things that are not as they were. For example, when he changed Abrams's name to Abraham, Abraham means father of nations. When Abraham and Sara had no children, he changed Sarah's name from Sarai to Sarah. Sarah means mother of nations. God told Abraham to look up to the sky; his descendants would be like the stars in the sky. Lord, give us understanding and knowledge of Your will and ways. There is so much I could say, but I will stop for now. God bless and keep you blessed. God has, through the years, answered so many prayers to meet needs and still is meeting the needs of others. Again, God bless and keep you!!!

If it ever was a time before that we needed to seek the kingdom of God first, and everything else will be added unto us, it is now.

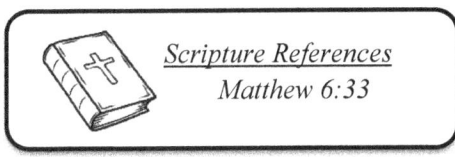

We must take a stand for righteousness and holiness like never before and learn to be obedient to the Word of God. We must obey God first in prayer and confess God's Word. We acknowledge God's Word when building our faith and confessing it in faith.

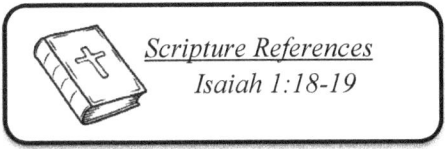

Meditate on God's Word day and night, then we shall have great success.

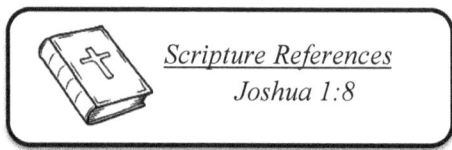

Scripture References
Joshua 1:8

I heard something this week from Dr. Tim Sheets. It confirmed what I saw in the spirit. I was at a prayer meeting in Tulsa and saw more people praying than I could imagine. There were a lot of people interceding. It's the same thing he saw. God's glory will cover this earth as the waters cover the sea. There are realms of glory in the Holy Spirit. I have been in powerful revivals in churches in my home state.

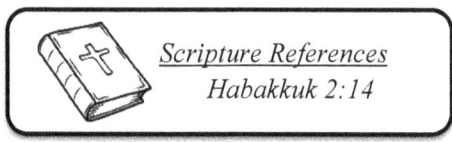

Scripture References
Habakkuk 2:14

In the first sermon I preached in the church, a Pastor asked me to minister to the youth. Somebody was behind me, giving me what to say. I turned around, and there was no one there. But the heavens were opened. When I finished ministering, the power of God got stronger. I knew Jesus was in that place. I kept saying I wanted to touch you, Jesus. I kept reaching for him. That was one of the most powerful times of ministry I had at that time.

Something remarkable happened in that meeting. Apostle Louis Greenup Church had a revival that used to have service every night, and the glory was so powerful in that church. I got the Holy Ghost in that church around one or two in the morning. The Holy Ghost fell on me before the pastor's wife could get the word out of her mouth. The Holy Ghost picked me up and sat me back down, and I don't remember when I got on the floor, but I was hovered down on my face, speaking in other tongues. I remember saying the exact words over and over. I still remember those words today. We're getting ready to see angels minister like never before to help us carry out this gospel to finish the great commission with mighty miracles, signs, and wonders. Jesus said greater works than these things shall we do. God is building His army, and it's a mighty army; it will not fail.

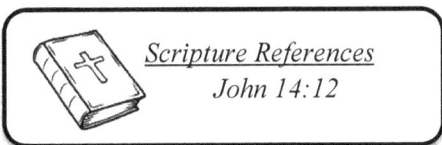

Scripture References
John 14:12

Many people will obey God, but many will hear God's voice who will not obey. God is speaking to His people, calling a fast and prayer, and the Holy Spirit will take over these meetings at a level they have never seen before. The glory of the Lord will fill all gifts of the spirit and move mightily. Some people are going to hear from the Lord. We must press in for the prize of the high calling in Christ Jesus. There are genuinely war angels I have had to use since I have been in Tulsa. The demonic spirit was so great. I think if I was in that realm, I could deal with and ask God for help and to send His war angels. I could remember when they came—the atmosphere changed. I could remember from that day forward. Things changed for then my health got better. As I continued to pray, my finances got better.

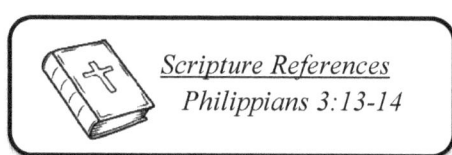

Scripture References
Philippians 3:13-14

I was still seeing people's lives changed for the better. I remember attending a revival and leaving to use the phone. While on the phone, I saw this young lady weeping. So I got off the phone and asked her what was wrong, and she was crying, so she almost couldn't talk. So I ministered to her from the overflow of the anointing upon my life. I asked her if she wanted to go to the revival. She said yes. Before the revival was finished, she went up to be born again. She gave her heart to the Lord. She told me while weeping that she was waiting to use the phone to get some drugs. What happened? The Holy Spirit arrested her. We will see a lot more of these as many of us walk with the power and authority of the Holy Ghost. God is going to do some extraordinary things. We are getting ready to see God do creative miracles; God will get the glory. God is going to move supernaturally. Miracles are going to be everyday things for the church.

Don't quit. Keep moving forward. Keep the faith. God will answer the prayer of His people. Keep calling on God to save your family and draw them closer to God. When I am saved, my whole household is saved. As for me and my house, we will serve the Lord. I choose life.

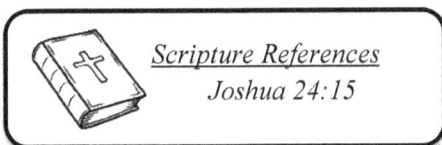

Scripture References
Joshua 24:15

The wealth of the wicked is laid up for the just. Keep yourself walking in the spirit and covered in blood. Make sure you repent. It is always God that causeth us to triumph in Christ Jesus.

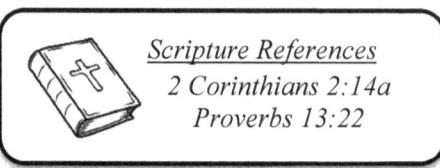

Scripture References
2 Corinthians 2:14a
Proverbs 13:22

Nay, we are more than conquerors through Christ Jesus in all things. We won!!

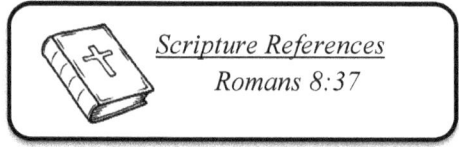

Scripture References
Romans 8:37

We overcome by the blood of the lamb and the word of our testimony. May the Lord bless and keep you. May He give you peace and cause His face to shine upon you. Remember to pray for America. Ask peace for Jerusalem.

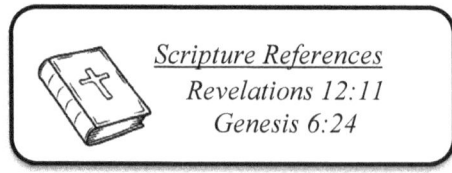

Scripture References
Revelations 12:11
Genesis 6:24

When Dr. Tim talked about revival and how great things in the church would happen during that revival, I agreed. All of the earth is waiting on the manifestation of the sons of God. God will do creative miracles.

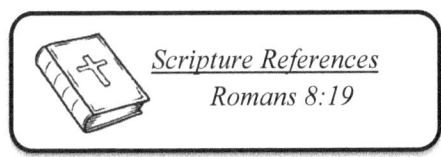

Scripture References
Romans 8:19

I had a conversation with the Lord about my car. I asked the Lord for a newer model car. Within two weeks, my car broke down suddenly. I was shocked because my current car was in good condition. My car was 26 years old, so I needed another car. Praise God it held up that long. God is good. I had no transportation. I continued to pray and thank God for my new model car. Two weeks later, the Lord supernaturally provided me with a lovely car! I am now driving around in my newer model car! Praise God. He will provide. He is Jehovah Jireh.

Salvation Prayer

Jesus died for our sins. There is no other way by which man can be saved. For God so loved the world that He gave His only begotten son so that whosoever believed in Him would not perish but have everlasting life. For all have sinned and come short of the glory of God. And only the blood of Jesus can wash away our sins. For all have sinned and come short of the glory of God. Jesus loves you so much that He died for you. Would you accept Him in your heart now? All of heaven is waiting on you. And believe that God raised Jesus from the dead and that He is the son of God and He is the way, the truth, and the life. Repent and turn away from your sins and receive Jesus. Now is the day of salvation. Ask him into your heart, and He will forgive you. And the angels in heaven rejoice over you. Welcome to the body of Christ, my sister, my brother. I am so excited for you. I encourage you to seek to be filled with the Holy Spirit and seek to find a good word based church.

About the Author

My name is Karen Neal. I was born in New Roads, Louisiana. I lived in Labarre, Louisiana, for a short time as a little girl. Then we moved to Pointe Coupee, Louisiana. My father and mother had eight children – four boys and four girls. I was the second oldest but the oldest daughter. My father was a farmer and a sharecropper. Daddy and Mama were people of integrity and hard workers. They taught us the same. They were some of the hardest-working people that I have ever seen. Daddy was a great farmer and a great gardener. Mama was right by his side. Mama was the most fantastic cook I know. Mama was also a powerful prophetess and prayer warrior. They taught us principles and were great parents. Daddy met a man from another city and got a good job in construction working with the union when I was thirteen years old. That was the year that my brother and I got baptized. After that, I sang in the choir at the church.

I am the mother of three lovely children, a grandmother, and a great-grandmother. I went to Southern University. I also worked at Southern University. I worked for a Fortune 500 company in

Personnel and did some modeling for their promotions. This was a great company; I did not want to leave, but I decided to leave to go to college. I do not regret my decision, but I would have loved to stay and work for this company. They did not want me to leave, but I got a better job. I trusted God to purchase a home. I worked in both positions, and God answered my prayers. As a single parent, I could buy a lovely home for my children and me. I was very young, but the hard work and studying paid off in the new job. I was around 30 years old and had three children. Praise God!

I also did political work for 20 years by petitioning and encouraging and educating the people to vote and the importance of voting. I also worked for the Federal Government. My job transferred, and I was moved to Tulsa, Oklahoma. I worked for them for about 20 years. To God be the glory. I also went to Bible college and attended Stephens Ministries. The word that was given to me by the pastor was, "Your gift will make room for you and put you before great men." To God be the glory!

www.ingramcontent.com/pod-product-compliance
Lightning Source LLC
LaVergne TN
LVHW061035070526
838201LV00073B/5053